Practising Grammar and Usage

Lois G. Reynolds
Pellissippi State Technical Community College

Judi Jewinski
Renison College
University of Waterloo

Prentice Hall Reference Guide
for Canadian Writers

Muriel Harris
Purdue University

Judi Jewinski
Renison College
University of Waterloo

PEARSON
Prentice
Hall

Toronto

ISBN-13: 978-0-13-515138-9
ISBN-10: 0-13-515138-4

Vice President, Editorial Director: Gary Bennett
Acquisitions Editor: Chris Helsby
Marketing Manager: Sally Aspinall
Supervising Developmental Editor: Suzanne Schaan
Production Editor: Amanda Wesson
Copy Editor: Valerie Adams
Production Coordinator: Avinash Chandra

1 2 3 4 5   12 11 10 09 08

Printed and bound in Canada.

PEARSON
Prentice
Hall

CONTENTS

Note that there are no exercises for Part One of the text (Question and Correct & Compare and Correct)

Part Two: The Writing Process

Part Three: Writing for Business and Other Purposes

Part Four: Style and Word Choice

Part Five: Revising Sentences for Accuracy, Clarity, and Variety

Part Six: Parts of Sentences

PART TWO
THE WRITING PROCESS

Chapter 1 Purpose and Audience

1a. Purpose

For each of the purposes for writing listed below, create a situation in which you might write with that purpose in mind. Identify, as well, the audience for whom you might be writing. Below is an example for the first purpose, "Summarizing."

EXAMPLE

Summarizing:

> I work for a consumer finance company, and my job is to look over an applicant's credit history—credit report, information from the application form, etc. I must summarize the credit history in a single paragraph for the loan officer who will make the final decision.

1. Summarizing:

   _____

   _____

   _____

   _____

2. Defining:

   _____

   _____

   _____

   _____

3. Analyzing:

   _____

   _____

4. Persuading:

_____

_____

_____

5. Reporting:

_____

_____

_____

_____

6. Evaluating:

_____

_____

_____

_____

7. Discussing/Examining:

_____

_____

_____

_____

8. Interpreting:

_____

_____

_____

_____

lb. Topic

To find a topic for a piece of writing, assume that an interviewer or reporter is asking you questions, to which you will write responses. An example of an answer to the first question is given below.

EXAMPLE

What is a problem you'd like to solve?

      Businesses downtown have lost customers to shopping malls. They need help.

1.   What is a problem you'd like to solve?

_____

_____

_____

_____

2.   What is something that pleases, puzzles, irritates, or bothers you?

_____

_____

_____

_____

3.   What is something you'd like to convince others of?

_____

_____

_____

_____

4. What is something that seems to contradict what you read or see around you?

_____

_____

_____

_____

5. What is something you'd like to learn more about?

_____

_____

_____

_____

6. What is something you know about that others around you may not know?

_____

_____

_____

_____

1c. Thesis

Narrow each of the following topics by asking yourself the series of questions listed with each topic. Then write the thesis that has developed from your answers. Analyze your thesis by underlining your topic once and your comment about it twice. An example is given here.

EXAMPLE

Topic: Carpentry

Who am I in this piece of writing?   I am someone with knowledge to share.

Who is my intended audience?   Readers of a do-it-yourself newsletter.

What is the purpose of this writing?   To inform.

What are some other conditions that   Length (space provided in the newsletter for this
    will shape this writing?   article),
                                                format, demographics of the audience (age, basic
                                                level of knowledge of carpentry).

Thesis:
Building an attractive and efficient computer desk can be an easy and affordable weekend project.

1. **Topic: Reality TV**

   Who am I in this piece of writing? _____

   Who is my intended audience? _____

   What is the purpose of this writing _____

   What are some other conditions that will shape this writing? _____

   _____

   _____

   Thesis: _____

   _____

   _____

2. **Topic: Human cloning**

   Who am I in this piece of writing? _____

   Who is my intended audience? _____

   What is the purpose of this writing? _____

   What are some other conditions that will shape this writing? _____

   _____

   _____

   Thesis: _____

   _____

   _____

3. **Topic: Fitness**

   Who am I in this piece of writing? _____

   Who is my intended audience? _____

   What is the purpose of this writing? _____

   What are some other conditions that will shape this writing? _____

_____

_____

Thesis: _____

_____

_____

4. **Topic: Solar Energy**

    Who am I in this piece of writing? _____

    Who is my intended audience? _____

    What is the purpose of this writing? _____

    What are some other conditions that will shape this writing? _____

_____

_____

    Thesis: _____

_____

_____

1d. Audience

In order to be sure that the information you write is helpful to your readers, consider more fully and carefully the general audience you targeted for the topics in the previous exercise. Analyze each audience by answering the questions below.

1. **Topic: reality TV**   Target audience: _____

    a.   What do the readers already know about the topic, and what new information will they need?

_____

_____

_____

_____

b. What is the audience's attitude toward the subject?

_____

_____

_____

_____

_____

c. What is the audience's background?

_____

_____

_____

_____

_____

d. What tone or level of formality should you use?

_____

_____

_____

_____

_____

2. **Topic: human cloning**   Target audience: _____

a. What do the readers already know about the topic, and what new information will they need?

_____

_____

_____

_____

_____

b. What is the audience's attitude toward the subject?

_____

_____

_____

_____

_____

c. What is the audience's background?

_____

_____

_____

_____

_____

d. What tone or level of formality should you use?

_____

_____

_____

_____

_____

3. **Topic: solar energy**   Target audience: _____

a. What do the readers already know about the topic, and what new information will they need?

_____

_____

_____

_____

_____

b. What is the audience's attitude toward the subject?

_____

_____

_____

_____

c. What is the audience's background?

_____

_____

_____

_____

d. What tone or level of formality should you use?

_____

_____

_____

_____

_____

_____

Chapter 2 Writing Processes and Strategies

2a. Planning

Use the planning strategies listed below to find material you might want to include in writing about the corresponding topics. An example of one planning strategy, "Brainstorming," is given here.

EXAMPLE

Topic: Whether to live in residence or off-campus

Planning strategy: Brainstorming

   deciding between residence and an off-campus apartment
     reasons to live in residence:
      □ close to classes
      □ paid up front
      □ includes meal plan
      □ meet more people
      □ more social activities

     reasons to live off-campus:
      □ more privacy/ more personal space
      □ lower costs
      □ get away from school
      □ noise level lower than residence

  checking out residence flyers
  checking out magazine articles on residence life
  visiting campus
  looking for possible roommates
  talking to friends and family
  knowing how much I can afford and not going above it
  searching apartment rental information
  reading classifieds

1. Topic: Saving money

  Planning Strategy: Brainstorming

  _____

  _____

  _____

  _____

2. Topic: Comparing dating conventions between two generations

    Planning Strategy: Freewriting

    _____

    _____

    _____

    _____

3. Topic: Fast food

    Planning Strategy: Listing

    _____

    _____

    _____

    _____

4. Topic: Violence in sports

    Planning Strategy: Clustering and Branching

    _____

    _____

    _____

    _____

5. Topic: How to plan a surprise party

    Planning Strategy: Outlining

    _____

    _____

    _____

    _____

6. Topic: Drinking and driving

   Planning Strategy: Who?—what?—when?—where?—how?—why?

   _____

   _____

   _____

   _____

2b–2c. Drafting and Organizing

Using one of the topics and planning strategies you completed in 2a, draft and organize a paper on that topic.

   _____

   _____

   _____

   _____

   _____

   _____

   _____

   _____

   _____

   _____

   _____

   _____

2d. Collaborating

Using one of the following methods, get responses from readers of the draft of the paper you completed in 2b-2c: meet with a writing-centre tutor, meet with a small group of students in your class, or meet with a writing group you form on your own. Ask your readers to respond to the questions below about your paper, and record their responses to each question.

1. What do the readers like about this draft?

    _____

    _____

2. What do the readers think is the main point of this paper?

    _____

    _____

3. Are there any sections that are unclear and need more explanation?

    _____

    _____

4. Does the paper fit the assignment?

    _____

    _____

5. Who is the appropriate reader or audience for the paper?

    _____

    _____

6. Are there any sections of the paper that seem out of order?

    _____

    _____

7. Are there any sections of the paper where the writing seems to digress from the topic?

    _____

    _____

8. Does the paper flow?

_____

_____

9. What else do your readers want to know about the paper's topic?

_____

_____

10. What is the most important revision to your paper your readers would suggest?

_____

_____

2e. Revising

Using the responses you gathered in 2d, along with the revision checklist for content and structure (p. 18), revise your paper for greater effectiveness.

_____

_____

_____

_____

_____

_____

_____

_____

_____

_____

2f. Editing and Proofreading

Using the Editing and Proofreading Checklist (p. 20), edit your paper for details of grammar, usage, punctuation, spelling, and other mechanics. Proofread your paper one last time for missing words, misspellings, and format. Then write the final draft below.

_____

_____

_____

_____

_____

_____

_____

_____

_____

_____

_____

_____

_____

_____

_____

_____

_____

_____

Chapter 3 Paragraphs

3a. Unity

Read the paragraph below, and then write a short paragraph commenting on its unity, describing what elements of unity are present or missing.

A recent expedition to Tibet resulted in the discovery of a previously unknown species of a small horse. The horses are only about four feet tall, but they are very strong. Expedition members experienced a great deal of bad weather during their stay in Tibet. Even though the discovery of the tiny horses caused much excitement in the scientific world, the local citizens seem to take them for granted and use them as pack animals.

_____

_____

_____

_____

_____

_____

_____

_____

_____

_____

3b. Coherence

Read the paragraph below, and then write a short paragraph commenting on its coherence, identifying what elements of coherence are present or missing.

Although many people think of the Canadian North as flat expanses of ice and snow, the geography of the area is actually quite varied. The Canadian North has long, cold winters and mild, short summers. The climate is actually quite dry, but most of the precipitation that does fall is in the winter and is in the form of snow. The area was home to forest-dwelling bands of aboriginal peoples historically.

_____

_____

_____

_____

_____

_____

_____

_____

3c. Development

Read the paragraph below, and then write a short paragraph commenting on the adequacy of its development.

> *Away from Her* is a brilliant film. It is directed by Sarah Polley and based on an Alice Munroe short story. It is critically acclaimed, so you know it's good.

_____

_____

_____

_____

_____

_____

_____

_____

3d. Introductions and Conclusions

1. Ask several classmates how they go about writing an introductory paragraph for a longer piece of writing. Write a short illustrative paragraph describing the different ways people draft an introductory paragraph.

_____

_____

_____

_____

_____

_____

_____

_____

2. Ask several classmates how they go about writing a concluding paragraph for a longer piece of writing. Write a short illustrative paragraph describing the different ways people draft a conclusion.

_____

_____

_____

_____

_____

_____

_____

_____

3e. Patterns of Organization

For each of the patterns of organization listed below, write a paragraph using that pattern on the topic provided.

1. Pattern of Organization: Narration

   Topic: An experience that taught you a valuable lesson

   _____

   _____

   _____

   _____

   _____

   _____

   _____

   _____

2. Pattern of Organization: Description

   Topic: A place where you go to think

   _____

   _____

   _____

   _____

   _____

   _____

   _____

   _____

3. Pattern of Organization: Cause and Effect

   Topic: Why you chose your current school

   _____

   _____

   _____

   _____

   _____

   _____

   _____

   _____

   _____

   _____

4. Pattern of Organization: Analogy

   Topic: The impact of the Internet on society

   _____

   _____

   _____

   _____

   _____

   _____

   _____

   _____

   _____

5. Pattern of Organization: Example

   Topic: Contemporary heroes

   _____

   _____

   _____

   _____

   _____

   _____

   _____

   _____

6. Pattern of Organization: Illustration

   Topic: Soap operas

   _____

   _____

   _____

   _____

   _____

   _____

   _____

   _____

7. Pattern of Organization: Classification

   Topic: Contemporary music

   _____

   _____

   _____

   _____

   _____

   _____

   _____

   _____

   _____

8. Pattern of Organization: Division

   Topic: Life on campus

   _____

   _____

   _____

   _____

   _____

   _____

   _____

   _____

   _____

9. Pattern of Organization: Process Analysis

Topic: Finding a job

_____

_____

_____

_____

_____

_____

_____

_____

10. Pattern of Organization: Compare and contrast

Topic: Two tourist destinations you have visited

_____

_____

_____

_____

_____

_____

_____

_____

_____

11. Pattern of Organization: Definition

Topic: Success

_____

_____

_____

_____

_____

_____

_____

_____

_____

Chapter 4 Argument

4a-4c. Writing and Reading Arguments, Considering Your Audience, and Finding a Topic

Choose a topic for a persuasive paper that is arguable, interesting, or of local concern. Once you have chosen your topic, decide on the appropriate audience for your topic, your purpose for the argument, the kinds of appeals you will use to make your case, and the common ground you share with your audience. If you have difficulty coming up with a topic of your own, you may choose from one of the following: smoking bans, Canada's international role as a peacekeeper, the validity of IQ tests, the benefits of bilingualism, work/study programs, anti-terrorist legislation, credit card fraud, or identify theft.

Topic _____

Audience _____

Purpose _____

Appeals _____

_____

Common Ground _____

_____

4d. Developing Your Arguments

1. Using the same topic for writing and the ideas you began planning in the last exercise, begin developing your argument by clarifying what your main point or claim is, what support you will offer for that claim, what warrants or unspoken assumptions are present in the argument, and what form of development (inductive or deductive) will be most effective.

Your claim _____

_____

The type of support you will use to convince the audience _____

_____

Warrants in the argument _____

_____

Method of development (inductive or deductive) _____

2. Consider how to avoid errors in reasoning in your argument by writing examples of logical fallacies about your topic that you would NOT use in a persuasive paper. By recognizing what you will <u>not</u> use as an argument, you will be better prepared to decide what you should use.

   a.   Hasty Generalization

_____

_____

   b.   Begging the Question (circular reasoning)

_____

_____

   c.   Doubtful Cause (post hoc, ergo propter hoc)

_____

_____

   d.   Using Irrelevant Proof to Support a Claim (non-sequitur)

_____

_____

   e.   False Analogy

_____

_____

   f.   Attack the Person (ad hominem)

_____

_____

   g.   Either …Or

_____

_____

h.   Bandwagon

   _____

   _____

3.   For more practice in logic, use the preceding list to identify the logical fallacies in the following statements or arguments. First, name the fallacy; then explain how the example illustrates that fallacy.

   a.   A vote for this candidate is a vote for environmental responsibility; a vote for her opponent shows a lack of concern for the environment.

      Fallacy _____

      Explanation _____

      _____

   b.   This candidate had a reported income of over $6 million last year. How can he possibly understand and help all the people in this country who don't have enough money to feed their children?

      Fallacy _____

      Explanation _____

      _____

   c.   I'm going to vote for this candidate because everyone who cares about the values I care about is voting for him.

      Fallacy _____

      Explanation _____

      _____

   d.   Assisted suicide, even though based on the desires of the person involved, should be illegal because anyone who wants to commit suicide is obviously incompetent and not capable of making rational decisions.

      Fallacy _____

      Explanation _____

      _____

e.   This candidate will not promote bilingualism. Throughout her career as an M.P. she has not learned French.

Fallacy _____

Explanation _____

_____

4e. Organizing Your Arguments

Decide upon the most effective organization for the argument you were developing above and justify why you have chosen that pattern of organization.

Pattern of Organization _____

Justification _____

_____

_____

(Now that you have completed Exercises 4a-4e, you should be prepared to draft, revise, and edit a persuasive paper on your topic if required.)

Chapter 5 Visual Argument

Develop a visual argument for each of the situations described below. Remember to consider these questions as you plan each visual argument:

- What claim do you want to make? (i.e., what is your point or thesis?)
- Who is the audience and what beliefs can you assume they have?
- What shared images can you draw on that will be immediately recognizable to the audience?
- How can you make connections between the claim and the images?
- Which images will have an emotional impact without overpowering the logic of the argument?
- Do you need a speaker to contribute ethical appeal?
- Is the image sufficient to be effective, or do you need carefully chosen words to enhance it?
- Are you avoiding obvious logical fallacies?

In the spaces below, describe (and draw if you wish) the image you would use.

1. As a teacher's assistant in a junior high school, you are asked to develop an image to persuade students not to begin (or to stop) smoking.

_____

_____

_____

_____

_____

_____

_____

_____

2. As an active student member of a political party, develop a visual argument to persuade successful, well-educated twenty-something professionals to vote in an upcoming election.

_____

_____

_____

_____

3. As an activist in your suburban neighbourhood, develop a visual argument to persuade your neighbours to have their pets neutered.

PART THREE
WRITING FOR BUSINESS AND OTHER PURPOSES

Chapter 6 Document Design

6a. Principles of Document Design

Group the information in the paragraph below into a list that will be less crowded and have more white space.

> The restaurant guide features lists of ethnic restaurants. It lists Chinese restaurants in the city. It also lists Italian, Middle Eastern, and Mexican restaurants. As a bonus, it lists ethnic restaurants by neighbourhood.

_____

_____

_____

_____

_____

_____

61b. Visual Elements

1. Put the information in the paragraph below into a **bar graph** to add interest to your webpage.

    > First-year students take an average of 20 hours per week. Second-year students take an average of 17 hours per week, and upper-year students take an average of 15 hours per week.

2. Now put the same information in a **line graph**.

3. List all the activities that you participate in on a typical weekday, say a Tuesday, during the term. Determine the number of hours you spend on each activity, and construct a **pie chart** that displays this information.

6c. Webpage Design

1. Draw a visual plan for a webpage for an online clothing store that would include the following pages:

   - Homepage

   - Men's clothing

   - Women's wear

   - Ladies' shoes

   - Children's clothing

   - Dresses

   - Clothing for toddlers

   - Children's sizes 5–10

2. If you have a personal website, retrace the steps you followed in planning it. If you do not already have a website, follow the steps below to begin planning one.

   a. Describe the purpose for your website (e.g., entertainment, persuasion, seeking employment).

   _____

   _____

   _____

   _____

b. Describe your homepage and/or draw a replica of it here:

c. Draw a visual plan for your website, showing the pages that will link to your homepage. Include as many
    levels as necessary.

6d. Presentation Format

Circle which of MLA or APA style each of the pages below belongs to.

1. Title Page   MLA   or   APA

2. First page, with author information   MLA   or   APA

3. Tables (on a separate page)   MLA   or   APA

4. Endnotes   MLA   or   APA

5. Works Cited List   MLA   or   APA

6. References   MLA   or   APA

7. Appendixes   MLA   or   APA

8. Figure Captions   MLA   or   APA

Chapter 7 Public Communications

7a1. Business Letters

Write a letter recommending a person for employment at the Overlands Development Corporation. The body of your text should contain at least two paragraphs. The person to whom you are writing is Phil Brannan, New Projects Director. The address is 128 Cedar Ave., Selkirk, Manitoba R1A 2G4. Send a copy to Monica Oden, Director of Human Resources. Your letter should be printed, not hand-written. .

7a-7b. Memos and Email Communications

Write a memo or an email about a situation or a problem that has arisen in the student club of which you are president. Explain the situation, and propose a solution. The correspondence should be addressed to the sponsor of the club. You may write your message below or type and print it for submission.

_____

_____

_____

_____

_____

_____

_____

_____

_____

_____

_____

_____

_____

_____

_____

_____

7d. Résumé Writing

1. Take the following Skills Résumé and reorganize it into a Reverse Chronological Résumé. Add dates as appropriate. The revised résumé should be ready to mail or email.

Donald Bryant

2155 Algonquin Ave.
North Bay ON P1B 4Z3
(705) 474-8216
dbryant@vista.ca

PROFESSIONAL OBJECTIVE

A career in hotel management involving guest relations, scheduling and vendor management.

EDUCATION

University of Guelph

Bachelor of Commerce in Hotel and Food Administration

GPA: 83.3%

Major-Related Courses:

Hospitality Management Fundamentals, Food Management, Supervisory Management, Hospitality Law, Seminar In Housekeeping Operations, Hotel Sales And Marketing, Advanced Hospitality Management, Front Office Management, Hotel Accounting

SKILLS

Accounting
- Student Council Treasurer
- Did bookkeeping for local hobby store (Hattie's Crafts)

Scheduling
- Events coordinator for HTMSA Student Council
- Scheduled work hours for UG book store employees

Vendor relations
- Worked with various food vendors at mall food court

WORK EXPERIENCE

Assistant Manager, Stone Road Mall Food Court; August 2007 to present

Assistant Manager, College Bookstore; Fall 2006 to Spring 2008

2. Type a cover letter to accompany the revised résumé.

Chapter 8 Writing for Oral Presentations

1.   Outline and develop a brief oral presentation based on a paper or a project that you have already written. Begin by identifying the following:

      a.   Your purpose for making the presentation:

      _____

      _____

      b.   Your audience:

      _____

      c.   Your main point (your thesis):

      _____

      _____

2.   Now prepare the following visual aids, which you can present as overhead transparencies or slides. Be sure to keep the text uncluttered and include lots of white space:

      a.   Title

      b.   Outline

      c.   2– 4 content slides (include at least one graphic or diagram)

      d.   Contact information

Chapter 9 Writing about Literature

9a. Ways to Write about Literature

Read a play, a poem, a novella, or a short story. Briefly describe the following aspects of the work:

1. **Plot**—How do events connect? Do some events foreshadow others?

    _____

    _____

    _____

    _____

    _____

    _____

    _____

    _____

2. **Characters**—Who is the main character in the work? Does this character change? If so, how?

    _____

    _____

    _____

    _____

    _____

    _____

    _____

    _____

3. **Narrative Structure**—Do the events proceed in chronological order? What clues does the author provide?

_____

_____

_____

_____

_____

_____

_____

_____

_____

4. **Narrator**—Is a character telling the story? If so, how does this affect how we see the action? If not, how much are we shown (thoughts, movement in place, time, etc.)?

_____

_____

_____

_____

_____

_____

_____

_____

_____

5. **Gender**—How does the work portray men and women? Is there a difference in how each is portrayed?

_____

_____

_____

_____

_____

_____

_____

_____

6. **Genre**—Name what category of literature characterizes this work: comedy, tragedy, romance, science fiction, horror, fantasy, gothic, and so on. Explain how it fits.

_____

_____

_____

_____

_____

_____

_____

_____

9c. Literary Terms

Define each of the following:

1. Genre _____

2. Imagery _____

3. Metaphor _____

4. Plot _____

5. Setting _____

6. Symbol _____

7. Theme _____

9d. Conventions in Writing about Literature

Next to each example below, identify the verb tense that should be used.

1. A biography of the author _____

2. A brief summary of a short story _____

3. Introducing a line from a poem _____

4. Describing the environment in which a novel was written _____

Chapter 10 Writing Examinations

1.   Consider the central topics of one of the courses you are currently taking. Imagine three different questions that might be asked on a final exam in this course, and record these below. Underline the verb that identifies how the marker expects you to develop your answer.

a.   _____

_____

_____

b.   _____

_____

_____

c.   _____

_____

_____

2.   In the following instructions for a short answer question, fill in the blank with a topic from a course you have studied. Then answer this question in a brief paragraph.

Identify and explain the significance of _____.

_____

_____

_____

_____

_____

_____

_____

_____

PART FOUR
STYLE AND WORD CHOICE

Chapter 11 Precise Words

11a. Denotation and Connotation

1. Each of the following words has either a positive or negative connotation. Think of a corresponding term that has the opposite connotation.

EXAMPLE

devoted   obsessed

a. notorious   _____

b. assertive   _____

c. right-wing   _____

d. orderly, well organized   _____

e. custodian   _____

f. pre-owned automobile   _____

g. dirt   _____

h. fragrance   _____

i. meticulous   _____

j. failure   _____

2. Some connotations are personal and not always shared by others. Imagine positive or negative responses to the following terms, and write them here.

EXAMPLE

	POSITIVE	NEGATIVE
spider webs	glistening with dew on a summer morning	sticky and dirty in your hair after a trip to the basement

a.   water   _____   _____

b.   ice cream   _____   _____

c.   summer   _____   _____

d.   chemistry   _____   _____

e.   travel   _____   _____

f.   waltzing   _____   _____

g.   bleach   _____   _____

h.   sports cars   _____   _____

i.   exercise   _____   _____

j.   clouds   _____   _____

11b. General and Specific Words

1. The following paragraph contains some underlined general terms that need to be replaced by more specific terms. The paragraph also contains some underlined specific terms that need to be replaced by more general terms. Revise the paragraph by replacing these terms with more appropriate ones. Write your revisions above the underlined words.

People like driving up for fast food, and now so do their underline(animals). A new fast-food industry has begun

for drive-in dog food, and the menu is entirely for underline(spaniels and collies). These new underline(things) offer treats to dogs

with dog biscuits shaped to resemble food. The dog biscuits are made from foods that help keep dogs healthy.

The biscuits are underline(made to taste differently) so that dogs don't get tired of the same thing. Customers love the idea

of underline(driving their) underline(trucks to) a doggy drive-in after picking up their own underline(stuff). So far the menu has been limited to

dog biscuits, but underline(some people) will soon come up with new ideas for better underline(bone-shaped biscuits) for dogs.

2. The following descriptive paragraph contains some general terms and some specific terms. Underline these, and write G above the general ones and S above the specific ones.

Nobody could make soup like Grandmaman, probably because no one could ever assemble the ingredients so casually yet so confidently. Her stock pot was always full of leftovers from Sunday's dinner or Tuesday's lunch: chunks of chicken, a meatball or two, carrots, broccoli, or asparagus. These she would supplement with fragrant dried herbs from her cupboard and mysterious vegetable-flavoured waters collected in plastic margarine tubs from the back of her fridge. Nothing was ever wasted in Grandmaman's kitchen. It all went into the soup pot.

11c. Concrete and Abstract Words

The following paragraph contains some abstract words that are underlined. Change those abstract terms to more concrete ones.

When hikers reach a stream, they often decide to cross where the route approaches the water. But this may not be the best place at which to cross. Water usually moves most swiftly at the narrowest part of the stream. So, hikers should instead look for another spot where the stream widens. Here the current often has less velocity and may be easier to walk through. When hikers are carrying a backpack, they should loosen the shoulder straps and hip belt before immersion so that they can toss off the pack if difficulties occur. Some hikers find that if they suddenly hit a depression in the streambed, the weight of the backpack can toss them off balance. Another aid to crossing a stream is a good hiking stick. It can serve as another leg, offering better balance when there are dangerous elements present. It is helpful to remove unneeded clothing before crossing a stream with a swift current because the water can drag against wet outerwear. The hiker should also take each step slowly and deliberately. The forward foot should be planted firmly before the rear foot is moved. The careful hiker never hurries across a stream.

Chapter 12 Appropriate Words

12a-b. Standard English, Colloquialisms, Slang, and Regionalisms

Listed here are sentences that use some non-standard words, colloquialisms, slang, and regionalisms. Try to find a different way to express the same idea by writing a sentence using standard words in place of the non-standard and by using appropriate words in place of colloquialisms, slang, and regionalisms.

1. I sure ain't planning to take those guys to the big game.

   _____

   _____

2. Jason watched a sci-fi flick and then crashed on the sofa.

   _____

   _____

3. Nowadays you get stung for at least a toonie for a can of pop.

   _____

   _____

4. I'm not stressing about the English exam, but I'm pretty freaked about history.

   _____

   _____

5. The girls were blown away when they saw I got my tongue pierced.

   _____

   _____

12c. Levels of Formality

The following paragraph is written in a very informal tone. Revise it so that it is more formal and would be appropriate to print in a news magazine intended for a general audience of reasonably well-educated readers.

   People interested in tracing their heritage have a new gimmick. You used to have to depend on old photos or stories from grandpa. But those methods aren't foolproof. People forget dates, and old photos only get you so far. Now here's the latest rage. Scientists have come up with a sure-fire technique that is really cool, and many people are starting to get wise to the possibilities. All you have to do is get a sample of your DNA material, which tells you a ton about yourself and your ancestors. With just a swab from the inside of your cheek, scientists can follow your ancestors from where you are now, to whatever country they came from, all the way back to Africa, which is where they think human life began. This is called DNA "fingerprinting." The coolest thing is that all this information is already on your genes—you just have to find out! The only problem is that if you're a woman you can only trace the mother's information, because you don't have a Y chromosome. Only a man has it, so he's the one who has to trace that side of the family.

_____

_____

_____

_____

_____

_____

_____

_____

_____

_____

12d. Jargon and Technical Language

Listed here are some sentences that use jargon and technical terms. Try to find a different way to express the same idea by writing a sentence using easily understandable language for a general audience. You may want to use a dictionary to find the meaning of unfamiliar words and terms.

1. The physician admitted that the antibiotics he had prescribed for the inflammation of my gastrointestinal tract are counterindicated by over-the-counter cold medications.

     _____

     _____

2. The teaching associate facilitating our pottery-making class receives inadequate remuneration and benefits.

     _____

     _____

3. Our supervisor has requested that we revisit the problematic situation to provide input to its resolution.

     _____

     _____

4. A review of the paradigm suggests a strong correlation between academic achievement and commitment to educational pursuits.

     _____

     _____

5. A team of paleontologists is evaluating the ferromagnetic properties of multiple mesolithic artifacts.

     _____

     _____

12e. Pretentious Language

1. Listed here are some sentences that use what many people regard as pretentious language. Try to think of a different way to express the same idea by writing a sentence using plain English instead of the pretentious language. You may want to use a dictionary to determine the meaning of some words.

a. I ascertained that the oration I had planned to deliver to the assemblage of students unquestionably required substantial revision.

_____

_____

b. She was rendered mute by the import of the situation.

_____

_____

c. Nathan is an odd colleague who is noted for his singularity.

_____

_____

d. Resplendent in the brilliant rays of the early morning sun, the snow-draped evergreens sparkled in their luminous mantle of white.

_____

_____

e. The lucidity of the discourse was cause for significant veneration.

_____

_____

2. The language in the following paragraph is pretentious and wordy and thus inappropriate for most audiences. Rewrite the paragraph so that the language is appropriate for the target audience of students.

As the twenty-first century moves inexorably forward, institutions of higher learning are endeavouring to appeal to diverse student populations and provide unprecedented access to their resources by making education available in multitudinous formats. Participants may engage in scholarly pursuits in traditional classroom settings, or they may opt to complete an entire degree program without ever gracing a campus with their presence by conducting all their coursework in the amorphous environment of the internet. Online courses do not require the student's physical presence on campus and are conducted in their entirety through institutional electronic facilities. The student who is contemplating attempting this medium of intellectual pursuit must carefully consider the personal requirements for success in the online environment. The prospective online scholar must be highly disciplined, with no propensity for procrastination. He or she must

possess an elevated sense of personal responsibility and an advanced reading level. The preponderance of

evidence supports the contention that, contrary to the collective opinion of older adolescent computer literati,

online pursuit of academic credit is not facile and effortless. In point of fact, online classes indubitably require a

far greater investment of time and concentrated effort than traditional classes. Nevertheless, earning credit

through online educational opportunities will culminate in enhanced computer literacy as well as discipline-

specific erudition.

_____

_____

_____

_____

_____

_____

_____

_____

_____

_____

_____

_____

_____

_____

_____

_____

_____

_____

12f. Clichés

Listed here are some phrases that many people regard as clichés. Try to think of a different way to express the same idea by writing a sentence using fresher language.

1. dumb as a post

_____

_____

2. rain or shine

_____

_____

3. beat around the bush

_____

_____

4. easier said than done

_____

_____

5. too good to be true

_____

_____

6. work the fingers to the bone

_____

_____

7. fast and furious

_____

_____

8. first and foremost

    _____

    _____

9. back in the day

    _____

    _____

10. move at the speed of light

    _____

    _____

12g-h. Offensive Language and Inclusive Language

1. The following paragraph has some language that can be revised. On the lines below, rewrite the paragraph to eliminate potentially offensive wording, and underline all the changes that you make. You may need to make other changes as well.

    In many suburban housing developments built during recent decades there are homeowners associations that enforce housing codes on all the homeowners. The average owner in such a suburb may think that he is free to paint his house whatever colour he likes or park any kind of car in his driveway, but that is not the case. Homeowners associations often have a lawyer who spends his days enforcing the laws enacted by these associations. The laws see to it that all the members abide by the group's standards of good taste. No plastic flamingos or garden gnomes are allowed on the lawn, and every house painter who works in the suburb knows that he cannot use certain colours for house trim, such as bright pink or a gaudy yellow, because he has to follow community guidelines. When houses are built in new developments, there are usually restrictive covenants that force the buyer to join the association, whether he likes it or not. Even when someone challenges the laws, he usually loses as the covenants are legally binding. It all starts with the builder because when a builder builds, he wants to make certain that the land value for the community stays high so that he can continue to sell his houses at a good price. The builder often starts off as the chairman of the homeowners association so that he can guide the formation of the rules and regulations. In one exclusive community in the States there are even regulations for local government and civil servants, including dress codes for policemen, taxi drivers, and mailmen. The only challenges that have gotten through the courts are those that show some regulation discriminates on the basis of race, religion, sex, or other characteristics of the homeowner.

_____

_____

_____

_____

_____

_____

_____

_____

_____

_____

_____

_____

_____

2. Write a paragraph about a job you have had or about the career you hope to pursue when you have graduated. Write the paragraph in third person, not in first person, and include a description of the responsibilities and expectations of anyone in that job. Be sure to use inclusive language in your description.

_____

_____

_____

_____

_____

PART FIVE
REVISING SENTENCES FOR ACCURACY, CLARITY, AND VARIETY

Chapter 13 Sentence Variety

1. Identify each of the following sentences according to the letter that describes it.

    a. simple sentence (one independent clause)

    b. compound sentence (two or more independent clauses)

    c. complex sentence (at least one independent clause with at least one dependent clause)

    d. compound-complex sentence (at least two independent clauses with at least one dependent clause)

    e. incomplete sentence (does not have at least one independent clause)

____ 1. In today's society many working people who are in their thirties or forties face the problem of providing

        care for both their children and elderly parents while they are at work.

____ 2. Since children have less contact with older people than in previous generations, a growing number of

        programs are being designed to bring children and older people together.

____ 3. Which will benefit both groups.

____ 4. The sandwich generation, as the middle generation is called by the media, is fortunate that there are such

        programs.

____ 5. In some programs, there are centres for child care next to centres for the elderly, and there are plenty of

        opportunities for visiting between the centres.

____ 6. Including shared activities such as cooking and birthday parties and informal get-togethers for storytelling

        hours.

____ 7. Psychologists point out that this kind of contact, even between old people and youngsters who are not

        related, can fill a void in young children's lives when they do not have a grandparent living nearby.

____ 8. In addition, companionship with children keeps older people from feeling isolated and lonely.

___ 9.   There is also a societal need for older people to transmit life experiences to younger generations.

___ 10. Something that is becoming increasingly less frequent in our mobile society where children move away

from their parents and raise families on their own.

___ 11. Programs to link children and the elderly have been so successful that similar programs have also sprung up

that link retirees with at-risk teenagers, and these programs are providing great benefits as well.

2. The following paragraph has monotonous sentence structure. Revise the paragraph by using a combination of
strategies to add variety.

      Animal rights activists are known primarily for their campaigns against fur coats and the use of animals

in laboratories. Now they are also campaigning against the rodeos at the Calgary Stampede. The Stampede is

the world's largest rodeo. Protestors say that rodeo animals are being mistreated. They cite numerous deaths of

horses and cattle during the Stampede. Animal rights activists say that rodeo horses buck because they are in

pain and that even accidental death of these horses is abuse. Rodeo cowboys say that this is not so. Deaths are

rare, and the owners make efforts to take care of their horses. The animals are well fed and comfortable. The

animals are treated like star athletes. They enjoy performing. Animal rights activists also condemn calf roping,

as in the past years several calves have been hurt. Roping breaks calves' necks. It can also snap vertebrae and

legs. Eliminating calf roping could mean an end to the rodeo part of the Stampede. Stampede enthusiasts argue

that this would end a long-standing tradition. Most animals are not harmed. Animal rights activists say that a

tradition that harms animals is barbaric. Organizers point out that there are thorough investigations whenever

any animal is injured at the Calgary Stampede. They invite activists to join the over one million spectators each

year. Then they would see for themselves.

_____

_____

_____

_____

_____

_____

3. Using at least one of each sentence type (simple, compound, complex, or compound-complex), write a paragraph of five to seven sentences. You may wish to write about animal rights or animal activists. Label your sentences.

4. Find a paragraph you have written previously that you think needs more sentence variety. Rewrite the paragraph here so that you have combined sentences; added words, phrases, or clauses at the beginning of the sentence; or changed some sentences to dependent clauses within the sentence.

_____

_____

_____

_____

_____

_____

_____

_____

_____

_____

_____

_____

_____

5. The sentences in the following paragraph are all short, simple sentences, so the paragraph is choppy and unsophisticated. Improve the style and sense of the paragraph by adding sentence variety, combining the sentences with coordination and subordination, and adding transitions as needed.

Gardening can be a worthwhile activity. The gardener can produce food for her family. She can also help to save the environment and prevent the overuse of landfills. One way to do this is by mulching. Mulching is actually recycling. The gardener can recycle grass clippings and leaves. The clippings are from mowing the yard. The leaves have to be raked in the fall. The clippings and leaves are usually gathered in plastic bags. The bags are taken to the landfill by the waste collection companies. The gardener can use scraps from the kitchen. These scraps are usually discarded into plastic garbage bags also. The gardener can collect clippings and leaves in a corner of the garden. She can add scraps of food to the clippings and leaves. She can mix these all together to provide organic mulch. This mulch can be spread on the garden. The mulch will provide nutrients for the soil. The nutrients will cause the garden to produce bigger and better vegetables. The gardener reaps many rewards from her activities.

_____

_____

_____

_____

_____

_____

_____

_____

_____

_____

_____

_____

Chapter 14 Comma Splices and Fused Sentences

The following paragraph contains some sentences that are punctuated incorrectly, some comma splices, and some fused sentences. Correct all the punctuation errors.

Where Canadians in the '60s were known as a nation of savers, nowadays we seem to be encouraged to spend as much as possible as quickly as possible. This attitude is expressed on television advertising also plays on this appeal. Many see a relationship between these current attitudes and gambling on lotteries, it is easy to understand why more and more people are handing their money over to chance, fate, and luck if what they are looking for is instant gratification. Statistics show this attitude is growing, in the late '80s, lotteries grew an average of 17.5 percent annually—roughly as fast as the computer industry. High-tech advertising for the lotteries takes attention away from the fact that a player has virtually no chance of winning, advertisements focus instead on the fantasy of what it would be like to win. Surveys conducted by lotteries show that few players have a clear understanding of how dismal their odds of winning really are, a player has a better chance of being struck by lightning than of winning a lottery.

Chapter 15 Sentence Fragments

1. The following paragraph has both fragments and complete sentences. Identify each one as either a fragment or a complete sentence.

(1) A fierce battle has developed in Canadian schools over the question of sexual education. (2) Until recently, teaching about "the birds and the bees" was the parents' job. (3) Whether parents would teach their children about sex or not. (4) But for many, sexual education in schools is an important way to decrease teen promiscuity. (5) That learning about sex without the moral or emotional consequences is unhealthy and will lead to further promiscuity. (6) But others say that teens who do choose to become sexually active are more aware of birth control and protecting themselves from sexually transmitted diseases (STDs). (7) That teens are less likely to engage in sexual activities when they know about their choices. (8) The current compromise in most provinces is for schools to offer sex education but to allow parents to remove their children if they so desire. (9) Some see it as worrisome that children are learning about sexuality. (10) Although others say that the more information their children have, the better. (11) This dispute shows the divide in Canadian families and their view of sexuality.

1. _____

2. _____

3. _____

4. _____

5. _____

6. _____

7. _____

8. _____

9. _____

10. _____

11. _____

2. Revise the sentences you identified above as fragments so that they are complete sentences. Write the number from the list in the previous exercise; then rewrite the sentence.

_____

_____

_____

_____

_____

_____

_____

_____

_____

_____

_____

_____

_____

_____

_____

_____

_____

Chapter 16 Coordination and Subordination

1. The sentences in the following paragraph can be improved by paying attention to coordination and subordination. Rewrite the paragraph to establish better connections while avoiding excessive or inappropriate links.

We are movie addicts. Over 75 percent of all households now have DVD players, so hotels hope to make their guests feel at home by providing equipment for watching movies of their choice. Some of the largest hotel chains have added DVD players in the rooms which can be used by renting DVDs from shops in the hotel where there is a good selection of recent movies for guests to view in their rooms. In these hotels guests can show their room card and can rent a movie at a reasonable rate. Other hotels don't want to bother with stores in the lobby, and they are exploring a different option, so they are adding automated video dispensing machines in their lobbies that hold hundreds of titles and have new releases as well as standard favourites. One hotel chain has a lot of large business conventions, and it has investigated another approach. It is offering to distribute to guests DVDs that the corporation holding the convention wants its participants to see since corporations like this because the DVDs can convey some of the key ideas being presented at the convention. DVD players in hotel rooms may soon be standard equipment, just as television sets were added years ago when we became addicted to television so that guests expected to be able to watch televisions in their hotel rooms.

_____

_____

_____

_____

_____

_____

_____

_____

_____

_____

_____

_____

_____

_____

2. Rewrite the groups of sentences below into single sentences through coordination and subordination.

a. Junk food is low in nutritional value. It is high in price. People buy a lot of it anyway.

_____

_____

_____

b. Children with disabilities deserve special attention. They get this attention from schools. They get this attention from their teachers. The teachers are specially trained to work with them. They get this attention from their peers.

_____

_____

_____

c. It has been a terribly cold winter. People have been feeding ducks. The ducks have had trouble finding food.

_____

_____

_____

Chapter 17 Parallel Constructions

1. In the following paragraph, underline all parallel constructions, and revise any non-parallel forms.

Recently, two pilots, one in a 175-seat commercial airliner and with the other one in a small, twin-engine corporate jet, were barrelling toward each other. On the instrument panel of the commercial jet, a small air traffic screen flashed a yellow circle and a voice announced, "Traffic." As the yellow circle approached the centre of the screen, it changed to a red square. The voice said loudly, "Climb, climb." Noticing the red square and as he pulled up, the pilot saw the other craft fly past several hundred feet below. The voice that called out the warning was not the co-pilot but the latest audiovisual aid to arrive in cockpits of planes, a traffic alert and collision avoidance system called ACAS (Airborne Collision Avoidance System). Transport Canada modified the Canadian Aviation Regulations in 2007 and issuing an order requiring that the ACAS system be mandatory for all newly manufactured airplanes in Canada and that all commercial airplanes meet the standards within two years. The system works by computing the distance between planes, warning planes when they get within six miles of each other, and then to decide which plane should climb and which should descend to avoid a collision.

2. Use the following connectors to write sentences on the topic of transportation safety.

a. neither/nor _____

_____

b. not . . . but _____

_____

c. not only/but _____

_____

d. whether/or _____

_____

e. both/and _____

_____

Chapter 18 Sentence Clarity

1. The following paragraph has some clarity problems. Revise the paragraph to make meanings clearer.

      To jot handwritten notes onto an electronic pad may be a new approach to using computers. A special pen that projects a narrow light beam onto the pad is the way this is done. For computer users who have had to rely on entering data into a computer by means of a keyboard, it is a major step forward in using computers. Not having to type is less distracting to many people who are not skilled typists but whose computer usage is high. It has been the goal of computer developers to rid the computer of keyboards for the last twenty-five years. But there has been insufficient development in the field of character recognition as this is necessary for the elimination of keyboards. Teaching computers to read through optical character recognition is one way to eliminate the keyboard. Recognition of the human voice is another way for computers to cease to rely on keyboard inputting of data. Speech recognition is not advancing as rapidly as some computer developers would like, and it is not likely that the near future will see computers we can converse with. We hardly have not appropriate technology that is this advanced. More promising is the ability of the computer to scan images. Already character recognition machines are being used in offices where pages of printed material are scanned by machines. Also under consideration by computer developers are electronic gloves that could be used by people to point to areas of the screen. There is hardly no limit to what will be coming next in computer development. The doing away of the keyboard will result in saving time and in the elimination of all the typographical errors.

_____

_____

_____

_____

_____

_____

_____

_____

_____

_____

_____

_____

_____

_____

_____

2. Write a paragraph of at least five sentences in which you draw arrows from old information in sentences to new information. Use positives instead of negatives, avoid double negatives, and make a special effort to use verbs instead of nouns. Underline any passive voice verbs, and make sure that they are appropriate. You may want to write about your experience with computers.

_____

_____

_____

_____

_____

_____

_____

_____

_____

_____

_____

_____

Chapter 19 Transitions

1. Rewrite the following paragraph by using transitions to build bridges between the sentences and parts of sentences. Underline the transitions you've added in your revised version.

My father really needs help. He is a workaholic. He works nearly fourteen hours a day. Doctors have told him it is bad for his health. It is affecting his family. He has worried my mother to no end. My family has tried to help him. He has not acknowledged the problem. He has a commitment to his company that is hard to imagine. He sneaks out of the house before anyone is awake. He gets home after most of us have finished dinner and are getting ready for bed. He works at home. His computer is connected to the one at his office. His work calls him at home. He has a pager and a cell phone. Things may be getting worse. Dad accepted a promotion to regional director.

_____

_____

_____

_____

_____

_____

_____

_____

_____

_____

2. Write a paragraph of at least five sentences that you connect by the deliberate use of transitions. Underline these. You may want to write about your experience with delays in grocery store checkout lines.

_____

_____

Chapter 20 Sentence Economy

1. The following paragraph contains many words and phrases that are unnecessary. Edit the paragraph to make it more concise, and then rewrite it on the lines below.

It is definitely true that, as we all know, the topic of telling time is one that is of great importance to us all. This paragraph will discuss here the topic of time in our daily lives and how the concept of time has changed over time through the ages. Time plays an important role in people's lives because it is the essential measure against which other measurements of great and necessary importance were made. For example, we know that we can see that we measure the heart rates of our bodies in terms of time, and we know that we measure how fast our cars travel in terms of time. We organize our days and nights into whole segments of time, such as days, hours, minutes, and seconds, and from the very earliest beginnings of civilization people have counted the passage of time in terms of counting sunrises and sunsets or the movements of the moon as well as the movements of the sun in the sky overhead. For many centuries there was speculation about the nature of time that was mostly a philosophical discussion of how people perceive time and experience the passage of time. But in the twenty-first century science of today, since the work done by Albert Einstein, physicists have now come to realize that time is a definite dimension of the physical universe. Time is a measure of motion in space, not just some philosophical or theoretical thing that exists in people's minds as a concept they think about. The work of Albert Einstein, who was a physicist, also showed that time is not an absolute thing and that there is no such thing as a unique absolute time. It is known that people used to think that any event measured in time would be seen to take the same amount of time. To give an example of what this means, people used to think that two good clocks which are in good, accurate working order would agree on the time interval that it takes between two events. But history books tell us that the discovery that the speed of light appeared the same to every observer, no matter how he or she was moving, led to the theory of relativity. Now we know that time is seen by everyone relative to the observer who measures it. Each observer who observes time can have his or her own measure of time as recorded by the clock that he or she carries. Clocks that are carried by different observers do not necessarily have to agree. This view that observers do not have to agree on the time interval is a very different view of time from the older view of time that it is an absolute thing. However, as has been shown here, even with this notion that time is not an absolute thing, we still in our lives today rely on time as our primary means of measuring how long it takes to do something.

_____

_____

_____

_____

_____

_____

_____

_____

_____

_____

_____

_____

2. The following is characterized by wordiness and trite language. Rewrite the paragraph on the lines below to make it concise and precise.

       Many people in this day and age are completely devoted to their pets that they think they cannot live without. People particularly seem to feel this way about their dogs, although it is certainly likely that some people feel that way about cats too. Whether the pet is a gigantic mastiff that looks wise as an owl or a big-eared Chihuahua that yaps all the time at everyone and everything it sees, all owners consider their precious pets to be their pride and joy. Reasonable, rational, thinking pet owners seem to be few and far between. Some people dress their pets up in expensive clothes so they look fit to kill. They may buy outfits and other pet paraphernalia on the internet or in fancy pet stores in upscale malls in big cities. They may even buy beds for

74

their pets. And many are the owners who send their pets to doggie daycares when they have to go to work.

These are people who would probably even take their pets to work with them if they were allowed to do that at

the place where they work. People who don't own pets may consider a friend who does own a pet to be crazy as

a bed bug because he or she spends so much money, time, and energy on the pet. But true pet lovers just can't

seem to face the drudgery of daily life without a pet. They feel more calm, cool, and collected when their pets

are there, so they are willing to spend an arm and a leg to keep their pets as content and happy as possible. And,

when all is said and done, who can blame them?

_____

_____

_____

_____

_____

_____

_____

_____

_____

_____

_____

Chapter 21 Consistency (Avoiding Shifts)

1. The following paragraph has a number of inconsistent shifts in person and number, in verb tenses, in tone, in voice, and in discourse. Rewrite the paragraph on the lines below so that it avoids any inconsistent shifting.

High school formals used to be dances where students dressed up in suits and dresses and celebrated their coming graduation, but now you have to spend big bucks for a tuxedo or elegant formal dress. Graduation has become big business as formalwear shops and limousine services offer their services in advertising campaigns. Tuxedo rental shops across the country report that grad dances, not weddings, account for the major portion of its business. One local shop owner said that he used to look forward to summer as his busy season because of weddings, but "now I make more money in the spring because of grad." The typical expenses now include the tuxedo rental, tickets, corsage, dinner, and limousine rental. You can easily spend $300 on the dance, and that was just for the basics. Graduates can spend additional funds for the latest fashions in tuxes, and photos can be purchased for $50 or more. Even when grad is over, there would be other expenses. Some kids go away for the whole weekend, often to a resort hotel. So you have to throw in the costs for a hotel, and if parents are invited along as chaperones, it is necessary to add in the cost of their rooms and meals too. High school graduates insist that this is all necessary as a rite of passage, but the expense is not appreciated by parents who often have to cough up a lot of the funds. And public school kids have started to jump on the bandwagon in a big way. Grade eight graduates now celebrate with expensive formal events as well.

_____

_____

_____

_____

_____

_____

_____

_____

_____

_____

_____

_____

_____

_____

_____

2. Write a paragraph of at least five sentences in which you pay special attention to consistency in pronoun person and number, verb tense, tone, and voice. You may want to write about leisure activities or favourite pastimes.

_____

_____

_____

_____

_____

_____

_____

_____

_____

_____

_____

_____

_____

_____

_____

_____

Chapter 22 Subject-Verb Agreement

1. In the following paragraph, underline the subjects of all the verbs.

Beloved of Canadian and international readers is one of the funny pages' most successful cartoonists, Lynn Johnston. Currently featured in over 2000 papers in Canada and abroad, Johnston's "For Better or For Worse" was first published in 1979. Everyday family issues like doing the dishes and trouble with school are turned into often funny, often heart-warming jokes by Johnston. Johnston planned to retire in the fall of 2006, but after being asked to reconsider by her publisher, she has made "For Better or For Worse" live on as a "hybrid-comic." The idea of the hybrid-comic is to combine new material with old comic strips, which are flashbacks to a different time in the life of the characters. If it is successful, Johnston may continue for years to come: her fans will get to follow the adventures of the Pattersons and their friends as they live everyday struggles. When will Johnston retire? It is too soon to know for sure, but for now her hybrid-comic is still keeping millions entertained.

2. In the following paragraph, underline the verb that agrees with the subject.

A business that is growing rapidly in popularity as well as in profits (is, are) selling meteorites to collectors, museums, universities, and research laboratories. The usual meteorite that dealers offer to customers (weigh, weighs) only a few grams or less, but sometimes, someone out collecting meteorites (find, finds) a piece that can weigh over 100 pounds. Either a whole large meteorite or some chunks (sells, sell) for thousands of dollars. But in some countries the government (is, are) beginning to pass laws that forbid the export of meteorites. None of these governments (want, wants) these national treasures to leave their countries. The price for meteorites (depend, depends) on the rarity of that kind. How much is known to exist (is, are) an important factor in determining the rarity of any specimen that is found. Of the three classes of meteorites, "irons"—made up of iron and nickel—are common, though they represent less than 10 percent of all meteorites that (strike, strikes) the Earth. But they survive the intense heat of entering the atmosphere better than other meteorites (does, do) and can be easily found with a metal detector. All other meteorites, which (is, are) made of stone, are the most common ones that are found. Among these there (is, are) some that may have come from nearby planets when meteorites hit their surfaces. Having a piece of Mars (is, are) a good way to start a collection.

3. As you complete the following sentences, make sure the verb agrees with the subject. For this exercise, use only a form of the verb BE in either present or past tense (am, is, are, was, were).

a. Elvis _____

_____

b. We _____

_____

c. Nearly all of my sister's clothes that she wears to school _____

_____

d. The store clerks and their manager _____

_____

e. Either Carlos or his brothers _____

_____

f. Not only the players but also the coach _____

_____

g. What I want to explain _____

_____

h. To feel successful _____

_____

i. Each _____

_____

j Some of the examples _____

_____

k. Some of the assignment _____

_____

l. The committee _____

_____

m. Cryogenics _____

_____

n. The scissors _____

_____

o. Acme Enterprises _____

_____

p. Her idea (complete this sentence using a linking verb) _____

_____

q. Magazine articles (complete this sentence using a linking verb) _____

_____

r. In the library, there _____ an interesting book on the history of television.

s. In the library, there _____ many books on the history of television.

t. It _____ his beliefs that formed the basis for his argument.

u. They are the people who _____

_____

v. She is the person who _____

_____

w. Mr. Baker is one of those instructors who _____

_____

Chapter 23 Mixed Constructions

23a.   Faulty Predication

1. The following paragraph has some sentences with faulty predication. On the lines below, rewrite these
    sentences so that they are correct.

    With the present concern for the environment, some companies are trying to increase their sales by

    advertising their products as environmentally safe. The makers of some plastic trash bags, for example, are

    claiming that their plastic is degradable. The reason for the claim is because there are additives that cause the

    product to break down after prolonged exposure to sunlight. Biodegradability, they assert, is when there is

    photodegradability, a breakdown by sunlight. But since most trash bags are buried in landfills, the benefits of

    photodegradability are questionable. Thus, the government has stated that one way to improve deceptive

    advertising claims is when they eliminate false or misleading information.

    _____

    _____

    _____

    _____

    _____

    _____

2. Finish the sentences for each of the subjects listed here. Pay special attention to avoiding faulty predication.

    a. The reason is _____

        _____

    b. Horror is _____

        _____

    c. His excuse was _____

        _____

    d. Her proposal was _____

        _____

81

23b. Illogical Comparisons

The sentences below can be improved by paying attention to the logic of the comparisons. Revise the sentences to make comparisons complete without being redundant.

1. Compared to my statistics class, I'm finding economics a lot easier. _____

    _____

2. We know that people who are regularly exposed to second-hand smoke are more likely to get lung cancer.

    _____

    _____

3. When I want to feel depressed, I compare the lifestyles of the rich and famous to myself. _____

    _____

4. After our small plane levelled out at 1500 metres, the flight became as smooth as any commercial airliner.

    _____

    _____

5. We are all convinced of the greater durability of Canadian products, even though they cost more to make.

    _____

    _____

6. What I've discovered in my interviews is that children under 10 tend to have musical tastes like their

    parents. _____

    _____

7. The Beatles have sold more albums than any musical group. _____

    _____

8. The features of one laptop are pretty much the same as every computer in the same price range.

    _____

    _____

9. There is no better time to observe mob behaviour than major sporting events. _____

    _____

Chapter 24 Dangling and Misplaced Modifiers

24a.   Dangling Modifiers

1.   Underline the dangling modifiers in the following paragraph.

The Library of Parliament has finally been renovated. Considered an architectural treasure, tourists love to see this perfect example of Victorian gothic style. The library is the only part of the parliament buildings to have survived the fire of 1916. During the renovation, the copper roofs have required specific attention, as they are considered to be national symbols. Weather-beaten and suffering from the elements, it was in the 1950s that work on them had last been done. Now a bright copper colour, chemical oxidation over the next twenty years will give the new roofs a familiar green tinge. Then, to protect the library from moisture damage, the roofs will have moisture barriers and a new drainage system. Though exposure to the elements cannot be prevented, the rebuilt roofs should fare better than their predecessors, thanks to modern technology. Looking better than ever, our Canadian heritage is well represented.

2.   Rewrite the sentences with dangling modifiers that you identified in the exercise above, eliminating the modifier errors.

_____

_____

_____

_____

_____

_____

_____

_____

_____

24b. Misplaced Modifiers

1. In the following paragraph, underline the misplaced modifiers.

The Canadian Food Inspection Agency has been recently busy with mad cow disease in its investigations. May 2003 saw the first case that Canada has reported in recent years. As a result of the findings, several ranches in Alberta, B.C., and Saskatchewan were quarantined as a precaution. At that time, 1,400 cows were nearly slaughtered so they could be tested for the disease. DNA evidence revealed that an infected cow had been born in Canada, so many countries, including the United States, banned the import of Canadian beef and dairy products in written declarations. Because of the Canadian Food Inspection Agency's aggressive program now, any cow has been destroyed that might have been exposed to the disease. Today, Canada is again considered a minimal-risk region for mad cow disease, and cattle sales are at home and abroad once again lucrative.

2. Rewrite the sentences you identified above, placing the modifiers appropriately.

_____

_____

_____

_____

_____

_____

_____

_____

_____

_____

_____

_____

_____

24a-24b. Additional Modifier Exercises

Identify the misplaced or dangling modifier in each sentence below and revise to correct the problem.

1. Being the first to use primitive tools, scientists have discovered Cro-Magnon man was more human than ape.

_____

_____

2. Mari stunned the pit bull with a large flashlight.

_____

3. After working at the dairy for twenty years, Jerome's dismissal was devastating.

_____

4. A lot of strength is needed to open a new jar of pickles.

_____

5. Brendan found an emerald woman's bracelet on the floor of the language lab.

_____

6. Looking for a quick way through the subdivision, the greenbelt offered a convenient shortcut.

_____

7. For the past three winters we have hardly had any snow.

_____

8. Kelly found a pie baked by her mother on the top shelf of the refrigerator.

_____

9. The township decided that nobody could dump anything at the landfill except local ratepayers.

_____

PART SIX
PARTS OF SENTENCES

Chapter 25 Nouns and Pronouns

25a-b. Nouns and Noun Endings

1. In the following paragraph, make the necessary corrections to nouns. In particular, make sure you add missing -s and -es plural noun endings and appropriate possessive markers. Underline your corrections.

       Sports fanatics are spending large sums of money these day to purchase sports memorabilia. In fact, says one of the industrys spokesperson, it is a $100 million-a-year obsession. Buyers look for scorecard, stadium seat, autographed baseball bat, puck, even children clothing that belonged to all-time greats such as Tiger Woods. One of Woods personal letter recently sold for over $10,000. Since Joe Lewis, a famous boxer, kept many of his old mouthguard, collectors are now paying over $2000 for boxed sets of Lewis mouthguard. There are plenty of website to keep collector informed about the availability of various item of interest. A sociology professor at a major university who has begun a study of this phenomenon reports that yearly increases in prices are staggering. One of the most valuable transaction ever was a 1979 Wayne Gretzky rookie card that sold for $80,000. In fact, Gretzky memorabilia is some of the most popular—and therefore the most expensive—sports treasure around. Prices can only keep going up since there are so many sports fanatic looking to buy.

2. Write a paragraph of at least five sentences and include nouns with -s and -es plural endings and nouns with correct possessive markers. Underline each such noun that you use. You may want to write about people who collect memorabilia.

_____

_____

_____

_____

_____

25c. Noun Phrases

For each of the following sentences, choose the letter that best indicates the function of the underlined phrase. Write the letter in above the phrase.

    a.   subject of the sentence

    b.   adds information about the noun it follows

    c.   acts as object of a preposition

    d.   acts as the object of the sentence

    e.   acts as a complement of a linking verb, completing the subject

1.   <u>Marketers</u> have been working on ways to improve aerosol dispensers so that they do not spray the harmful propellant into the atmosphere.

2.   One new product, an alcohol-free hairspray, cuts <u>emissions of chemical pollutants</u> by roughly 60 percent.

3.   For its propellant, this new hairspray uses dimethyloxide, <u>a non-damaging chemical</u>.

4.   <u>Reformulating a proven compound</u> can be expensive for manufacturers.

5.   Another solution to the problem is <u>a propellant-free container</u> with a rubber expanding sleeve.

6.   <u>The rubber's propensity to contract</u> provides the pressure to produce a spray when the nozzle is pressed.

7.   This new spray dispenser is already being widely used with <u>great success</u>.

25d. Pronouns

In the following paragraph, underline all the pronouns, including the personal pronouns, demonstrative pronouns, relative pronouns, interrogative pronouns, indefinite pronouns, possessive pronouns, reflexive pronouns, and reciprocal pronouns.

The business of sports collectibles has become so profitable that it has attracted con artists who manage to forge and sell bogus items. The forgeries have become such big business, in fact, that many con artists help one another and have developed a large network of bogus items. These items include fake Steve Nash signatures and imitation press box pins. Anyone who is in the memorabilia business can spot these as forgeries and fakes, but sports fans are often too enthusiastic to take the time to have their purchases checked by an expert. As a result, they often allow themselves to be conned. A lot of junk from people's attics is also cluttering the market. When someone finds yellowed pages from 1929 sports sections in her scrapbook, she may think she has an expensive treasure. Flea markets overflow with antiques which may or may not be worth anything. But if someone is willing to pay large sums of money, who can say whether that autographed photo or threadbare jersey is or is not a treasure worth collecting? With a market where buyers will pay over $1,000 for one of Sidney Crosby's old sweaters, it is worth it to clean out those old attics and scrapbooks.

25e. Pronoun Case

1. In the following paragraph, choose the correct pronoun in the parentheses, and underline it.

In 2004, Thomas C. Douglas was voted "the Greatest Canadian" on a nationally televised contest organized by the CBC. Tommy Douglas is considered a hero by (them, those) Canadians (who, whom) admire his idealism and commitment to socialism. (His, His') greatest accomplishment is probably that the NDP and (he, him) introduced universal public health care to Canada. However, Douglas was condemned at the time by doctors (who, whom) felt his plan was a disadvantage to (them, themself, themselves). Many doctors went as far as to say that Douglas intended to bring in foreign doctors (who, whom) the government would pay less but (who, whom) would offer lower standards of care. Canadians are also grateful for (he, him) for arranging to pass the Saskatchewan Bill of Rights, (which, what, that) broke new ground as it protected both fundamental freedoms and equality rights. He served as an MP and MLA, but Canadians remember (he, him) best as leader of the NDP. Douglas died of cancer in 1986 at the age of 81. Even now, many scholars continue to concern (theirselves, themselves) with the impact Douglas had on Canadian society.

2. Write your own sentences below correctly using the pronouns listed.

a. them

_____

_____

b. whom

_____

_____

c. his

_____

_____

d. yours

_____

_____

e. theirs

_____

_____

f. ours

_____

_____

g. her

_____

_____

h. me

_____

_____

i. who

_____

_____

j. your

_____

_____

k. us

_____

_____

l. I

_____

_____

3.   In the sentences below, underline the correct pronoun.

Fall break was over, and the research assignment was due the next day, so Ross asked Lucy if she wanted to go to the library with Amy and (he, him). The instructor had told the class that the students (who, whom) made high grades on the midterm exam would be those (who, whom) had read the assignments and completed all the homework. Ross had missed that lecture. When the girls and (he, him) reached the reference room, they saw several classmates (who, whom) they could work with. They asked their friends, "(Who, Whom) has finished the assignment?" They were surprised that all the other students were already finished and heading to Tim Hortons. It was clear to Ross that a long night lay ahead for (them, themselves). The next day, Ross asked the instructor, "Please give Lucy, Amy, and (I, me) one more day to finish the research assignment."

But the teacher said it wouldn't be fair to the rest of the students (who, whom) had all worked hard, so Ross and (they, them) learned the hard way not to procrastinate.

25f. Pronoun Reference

1. In the following paragraph there are some pronoun reference problems. Underline all the pronouns that do not have clear or correct antecedents.

When Benjamin Franklin discovered electricity in thunderclouds, he sparked a controversy that still has no clear answer. How do clouds become electrified in the first place? To this day they haven't been able to adequately explain how it contains such incredible amounts of electricity that a stroke of lightning can contain about 100 million volts. One researcher who wants to find some answers flies his plane into storms to measure electric fields and ice particle changes. It's bumpy work, he says, especially if there are large hailstones because it can damage the plane and the measuring equipment. On one trip they noticed that in sections of clouds where water and ice mix, the measuring devices picked up indications of strong charge separation. The answer may be that in a certain temperature range, the temperature can cause the charge separation. Another factor may be a kind of soft hail called "graupel," pea-sized particles that can look like miniature raspberries. They form when droplets of supercooled water collide, freezing together instantly. Ice crystals then bounce off the growing graupel, building up a charge from the friction just as you build up a static electricity charge when you scuff your feet across the carpet. When they are carried to different parts of the cloud, the result is a separation of the positively and negatively charged particles. Then, when the electrical difference between the ground and the sky becomes great enough, everyone should haul his or her kite in.

2. On the spaces below, rewrite the sentences from the paragraph above that have pronoun reference problems so that you eliminate all the pronoun problems.

_____

_____

_____

_____

_____

_____

_____

_____

_____

_____

_____

_____

_____

3. Write a paragraph of at least five sentences with correctly used pronouns in every sentence. Underline each pronoun and draw an arrow back to its referent (the noun to which it refers). You may want to write about natural phenomena.

_____

_____

_____

_____

_____

_____

_____

_____

_____

_____

Chapter 26 Verbs

26a. Verb Phrases

1. Underline the verb phrases in the following paragraph.

       Some scientists are saying that a buildup of carbon dioxide and other greenhouse gases in the atmosphere causes global warming. But another group of scientists argues that we should study the data more carefully before any firm conclusions are drawn. While scientists generally agree that an unchecked accumulation of greenhouse gases will cause changes, no one knows when it will start, how much will happen, or how rapidly it will occur. The most widely accepted estimate is that there will be a rise in the earth's average temperature as early as 2050. This could bring rising sea levels and severe droughts in some areas. But no one knows yet how clouds and the ocean's ability to absorb heat will affect this. When scientists understand this better, projections can be revised.

2. Write a paragraph of at least five sentences, and underline the verb phrases. You may want to write more about the greenhouse effect and global warming.

_____

_____

_____

_____

_____

_____

_____

_____

_____

26b. Verb Forms

1. In the following paragraph, use one line to underline verb forms that are part of the main verb and use two lines to underline verb forms that appear elsewhere in the sentence.

The evidence that global warming has started is not very strong. Some scientists believe that the concentration of carbon dioxide has increased over 25 percent since the early 1800s, but other scientists point to the fact that the average global temperature has risen by no more than a half degree Celsius. Even that rise is questionable since there was a cooling period from 1940 to 1970 that caused forecasters to predict a return to the ice ages. Therefore, to act on predictions by passing laws that restrict or ban the use of fossil fuels may be hasty; nevertheless, conserving energy, banning harmful chlorofluorocarbons, and planting more trees to absorb carbon dioxide from the air makes sense. Many industries are also acting more responsibly and are reducing hazardous emissions from their factories.

2. Write a sentence using each of the following verb forms as a modifier. In other words, they will appear elsewhere in the sentence than as part of a main verb.

   a. -ing verb

   _____

   _____

   b. -ed verb

   _____

   _____

   c. to + verb

   _____

   _____

26c. Verb Tense

1. Underline the correct verb tenses from the choices given in the following paragraph.

For over 130 years, future members of the RCMP (have attended, will attend, attend) a training program at Depot Division in Regina, Saskatchewan. From the outside, the RCMP headquarters (has looked, looks, is looking) like an ordinary building, but it (is, was, will be) considered a Canadian heritage site. Today, Depot (is considered, was considered, considered) one of the top tourist sites in North America. In May 2007, the Government of Canada and the Government of Saskatchewan (has opened, will open, opened) the multi-million-dollar RCMP Heritage Centre, which (has featured, will feature, features) several permanent exhibits about the history of the Mounties. The exhibit titles (included, will include, include) "Serving All of Canada, " "Cracking the Case," and "Duty Calls." Tourists (have been amazed, are amazed, amazed) at a sculptural procession called the "March of the Mounties," which runs the length of the main exhibit hall and (was, is, will be) 30 metres long. One of the main purposes of the Heritage Centre (is, was, has been) to educate Canadians about the role the RCMP (did play, will play, plays) in protecting our country and in creating the Canadian identity.

2. The following paragraph is written in the present tense. At the beginning of the paragraph, add the words "Last year" and change the verbs in the rest of the paragraph so that it is in the past tense. Be especially careful when changing irregular verbs.

Every year an average of 8,500 men and women write the RCMP entrance exam, but only 1,984 cadets are selected. At Depot, the RCMP training academy, cadets take part in an intense 24-week program, in both English and French. The cadets are divided into troops of 32 members. Together the cadets move through the program, which usually begins with scenario training and role play. The emphasis is on real-life situations. For that reason, much of the training takes place in a model detachment where cadets develop hands-on skills. Cadets act out arrests. Training also incorporates problem-solving, lectures, panel discussions, and community interaction. The program is gruelling, but once training is complete, cadets are prepared to begin their careers as RCMP officers.

26d. Verb Voice

1. The following paragraph contains both active and passive voice verb phrases. Indicate the voice by underlining "active" or "passive" in the parentheses.

Our nation's capital borders (active, passive) two provinces, Ontario and Quebec. Like many cities that are built (active, passive) on a river, the bulk of the population is divided (active, passive) on both sides. The bigger city is Ottawa, but over one-half of the city's employees reside (active, passive) in Gatineau, the city on the other side of the river. Problems are created (active, passive) when it comes time to finance projects that will benefit (active, passive) both cities. In 1959, the National Capital Commission was founded (active, passive) to organize such projects. Today, the NCC organizes (active, passive) projects that impact both Gatineau and Ottawa. Advocates of the NCC say (active, passive) that the organization makes (active, passive) events and tourism run more smoothly. Opponents claim that the NCC is a waste of money and that residents of Ottawa who pay higher taxes are taken advantage of (active, passive) by residents of Gatineau. Beautification of the capital region is a hot-button issue, with many people now advocating (active, passive) for the disbanding of the NCC.

2. Examine the sentences in the previous paragraph that you identified as having passive verbs. Rewrite them so that the verbs are in active voice or explain why the passive voice is more appropriate and less awkward.

_____

_____

_____

_____

_____

_____

_____

_____

3. Write a brief paragraph with at least five sentences in which you appropriately use three or more active verbs and appropriately use two or more passive verbs. Underline the active verbs once and the passive verbs twice. You may want to write about inventions that interest you.

_____

_____

_____

_____

_____

_____

_____

_____

_____

26e. Verb Mood

1. Some of the verbs in the following paragraph are declarative (express a fact), some are subjunctive (express some doubt or something contrary to fact), and some are imperative (express a command). Underline the mood used for each.

Singles bars and dating services are thriving (declarative, subjunctive, imperative), but there are always new approaches. In commercial dating services, one new approach that may be cheaper (declarative, subjunctive, imperative) than the standard videotaped interviews is the lunch-date service. For less than $50 a month, the company promises (declarative, subjunctive, imperative) three lunch dates a month. People are paired on the basis of simple criteria gathered from brief interviews that might last (declarative, subjunctive, imperative) less than five minutes. The company sets up the lunch date, and the participants take it from there. "Meet (declarative, subjunctive, imperative) new people," says the advertising brochure, "and enjoy (declarative, subjunctive, imperative) some interesting little restaurants." Since Statistics Canada puts (declarative, subjunctive, imperative) the number of never-married Canadians at 1.1 million and growing, these new twists on dating services may well prosper (declarative, subjunctive, imperative).

2. Write sentences using each of the verb moods listed below.

   a. declarative

   _____

   _____

   b subjunctive

   _____

   _____

   c. imperative

   _____

   _____

26f. Modal Verbs

1. The following paragraph includes modal verbs that express ability, a request, or an attitude (such as interest, expectation, possibility, or obligation). Underline the correct meaning from the choices given in parentheses after the modal verbs.

      When western products began appearing in Moscow, city officials worried that the signs and

advertising for these products might make (intend to make, could possibly make, need to make) Moscow look

less Russian. A law recently passed in Moscow warns that all stores and businesses must display (are capable of

displaying, expect to display, need to display) signs in Russian or at least change them into the Cyrillic

alphabet. This has caused many businesses to contact the city inspector because of questions they have. For

example, one businessman wondered whether he should change (has the ability to change, asks to change, is

obliged to change) the letters in the label for the Puma running shoes that he sells. He was concerned that

changing the letters from English to Russian might make (has the possibility of making, intends to make,

requests to make) the shoes less popular. The problem became confusing because the new law does not forbid

foreign words but does require the Russian sign to be bigger than the one in English. Different stores found

different solutions. An American cosmetics company, Estée Lauder, announced that it would put (was capable

of putting, strongly intended to put, was asking permission to put) one sign in Russian on the awning and

another sign in English in the windows. Despite all the questions and worries, the inspector in charge of enforcing this rule will be (is going to be, needs to be, may want to be) very strict about checking on foreign signs.

2. Write a brief paragraph with at least five sentences in which you use modal verbs (shall, should, will, would, can, could, may, might, must). Underline each modal verb that you use. You may want to write about problems in translating words from one language to another or about the difficulties of having to use the English alphabet to write words from a language that uses a different alphabet.

_____

_____

_____

_____

_____

_____

_____

_____

_____

_____

_____

_____

Chapter 27 Modifiers

27a. Adjectives and Adverbs

1. In the following paragraph, underline all the adjectives and adverbs, and then correct any errors in adverb and adjective forms by writing the correct form above the line. Do not include the articles *a, an,* and *the.*

> For many people, the crossword puzzle in the daily paper is one of life's little pleasures. Some say it is more like one of life's frustrations. While puzzle books conveniently include the answers in the back, newspapers usually print the answers in the next day's edition. Now there is a more quicker answer. Some publications have an automated solution. Readers can dial an 800 service for instant answers. This service is free to callers and is paid for by advertisers who sponsor each day's puzzle. The advertiser can run a small advertisement beside the puzzle or include a ten-second message that callers must listen to before the answers are given. Other newspapers handle this more differently. For their puzzles, there is a special number, and callers have to pay for all requests for clues. These services are actually a major breakthrough for frustrated puzzle-doers who have been used to waiting until the next day.

2. Write sentences correctly using each of the adjectives or adverbs below.

    a. clear

    _____

    _____

    b. clearly

    _____

    _____

    c. sure

    _____

    _____

    d. surely

    _____

    _____

e. badly

_____

_____

f. good

_____

_____

g. well

_____

_____

h. rapid

_____

_____

i. rapidly

_____

_____

j. real

_____

_____

k. really

_____

_____

l. hard

_____

_____

27b. Comparisons

Write sentences in which you use the correct comparative or superlative form of the word listed for the items given.

1. large

    items compared: two companies

    _____

    _____

2. large

    items compared: eight companies

    _____

    _____

3. exciting

    items compared: two movies

    _____

    _____

4. enjoyable

    items compared: three books

    _____

    _____

5. user-friendly

    items compared: all the computer software programs tested

    _____

    _____

6. good

    items compared: two music CDs

    _____

    _____

7. good

    items compared: three music CDs

    _____

    _____

8. bad

    items compared: all the meals you have ever eaten

    _____

    _____

9. far

    items compared: two cities

    _____

    _____

10. expensive

    items compared: all your course textbooks

    _____

    _____

11. old

    items compared: two sisters

    _____

    _____

27c. Prepositional Phrases

1. In the following paragraph, underline the correct choice for the preposition that should be used.

> It was once so normal to pour ketchup on everything that it was considered everyone's favourite condiment. Now salsa has replaced it as the preferred choice (among, between) the two (at, in, on) many restaurants. Salsa, which means "sauce" (at, in, on) Spanish, is defined as any fresh-tasting, chunky mixture, usually made with tomatoes, chilies, onions, and other seasonings. Although salsa used to be associated (to, with, for) Mexican cooking, it is now being used for a variety of foods not particularly Mexican. The popularity (of, about, to) salsa is apparently part of the current food trend as we become more interested (about, on, in) spicier foods. In 1988, only 16 percent of households (at, among, in) North America bought salsa. (In, At, For) two years, that figure was up to 36 percent, and the market continues to grow (in, at, by) a very fast rate. A marketing information company notes that salsas and picantes—which are different (from, than) salsas because they are thinner—account (on, to, for) about two-thirds of this market, a category that also includes taco and enchilada sauces. As the market expands, so do the choices. The simplest salsas are based (about, around, on) chopped tomatoes and chilies, and the types of chilies determine how hot the particular type of salsa is. Cookbooks with a variety of recipes indicate the preference of some people to make their salsas (in, at, to) home. Salsas are one of the few popular snack foods that are fat-free or nearly so, and many are made without preservatives, two characteristics that may contribute (on, to, around) their popularity now that people are interested (about, in) healthier eating. Riding on this wave of popularity are the new fruit salsas, made with peaches, pineapples, and so on, and vegetable salsas, made with pinto beans, corn, and black-eyed peas. Other varieties will surely appear as the market keeps expanding (in, on, at) the future.

2. Write sentences in which you correctly use the words and prepositions listed.

    a. compared to

    _____

    _____

b. compared with

_____

_____

c. independent of

_____

_____

d. similar to

_____

_____

e. different from

_____

_____

f. concerned about

_____

_____

g. used to

_____

_____

h. interested in

_____

_____

i. familiar with

_____

_____

27d. Clauses

1. In the following paragraph, underline the independent clauses, and put the dependent clauses in parentheses.

   If you are a sociable writer who lives in a big city and likes informal gatherings, you may want to join a local writer's club. A typical group might meet bi-weekly or monthly at a local Second Cup or Starbucks, where members can discuss their craft in comfort. Writers come from all professions; they can be doctors, professors, salespersons in shoes stores, tax attorneys, shipping clerks, or teenagers who write as a hobby and would like to improve. Others are professionals who have published a little or a lot but who still like to hear other opinions before they submit a manuscript. All of these writers share a love of the written word. Because they know how helpful it can be to get feedback, they willingly read each other's writing and offer constructive criticism.

2. In the following paragraph, underline the dependent clauses and identify them as adjective or adverb clauses.

   There are an estimated 50,000 magicians in North America. Most are amateurs who enjoy magic as a hobby. These amateurs often have elaborate equipment although their only audience is usually their friends and relatives. Some specialize in the small card, coin, and rope tricks that are always popular. Purists call this intimate "close-up" magic the only real magic because it relies so heavily on a person's manual dexterity. Because people seem to prefer to be fooled face to face, this close-up magic is also offered by professional magicians who perform at birthday parties and trade shows. One psychologist, who is also a magician, says that when something is done under people's noses, it's more magical. It's much more elusive. The spectacular effects of magic that is done on television don't seem to impress people quite so much. Whatever the cause may be, amateur magicians will keep buying those sponge balls, decks of cards, special coins, and paper flowers.

3. Write a paragraph of at least five sentences in which three or more sentences have dependent clauses. Underline the dependent clauses. You may want to write about magic or magicians.

   _____

   _____

   _____

   _____

_____

_____

_____

_____

_____

_____

_____

_____

27e Reduced Clauses

In the following paragraph, underline the reduced clauses. Then, on the lines below, write the original clauses as they would have appeared before being reduced.

One of the most deadly offensives for Canada during World War II was the raid on Dieppe, a sea-borne mission across the English Channel made by two Canadian brigades and other units. While being a British operation, the Battle of Dieppe, also known as Operation Jubilee, depended on almost 5,000 Canadian troops. After considering all the variables, one of the commanding officers, Lt.-Gen. McNaughton, claimed that chances for success were good, providing luck was on the side of the Canadians. This was not to be. Despite the fine weather, the troops, landing on the beaches around 5 a.m., met with a determined and well-organized counter-attack. By 9 a.m. they were beginning to lose ground badly after fighting valiantly. The decision was taken to retreat, evacuating any commando not already trapped behind the German lines. Of the Canadians making up the attacking force, 993 were killed, 586 were wounded, and 1,874 were taken prisoner. Long debated for its heavy cost in lives, the raid on Dieppe is still seen as a testament to Canadian bravery.

_____

_____

Chapter 28 Essential and Non-essential Modifiers

1. Underline the essential clauses in the following paragraph. Then, on the lines below, rewrite the paragraph by removing all the non-essential clauses and phrases and reinserting them as essential modifiers in the relevant sentence.

French teachers in elementary schools across Canada who want their students to speak more now have a new, groundbreaking program to help them. AIM, which students say is a lot of fun, is developed by a group of educators who want to introduce French in a way which will get the students involved. This program, which incorporates singing, story telling, and hand-gestures, is being used to get children to speak with ease. Students seem to enjoy the songs and stories, and the hand-gestures help them remember new vocabulary. At the end of a unit, students can put on a play that goes with the story for the rest of the school. Once students learn the vocabulary with confidence, teachers can use other exercises to expand the children's knowledge of French. AIM is rapidly growing, with over 3500 schools across Canada using it to teach French.

_____

_____

_____

_____

_____

_____

_____

_____

_____

_____

_____

_____

_____

2. Write a paragraph of at least five sentences in which at least three sentences have an essential clause and at least two sentences have non-essential clauses. Underline the non-essential clauses. You may want to write about ways to learn another language.

_____

_____

_____

_____

_____

_____

_____

_____

_____

_____

_____

PART SEVEN
SPECIAL GRAMMAR

Chapter 29 Writing in North America

If your first language is not English, write a paragraph describing how the writing style in your native language differs from the North American style. Issues you might consider in your paragraph include conciseness, topic announcement, organization, and source citation. If your first language is English, interview someone whose first language is different, and write a paragraph describing how that person's writing style varies from your own style.

_____

_____

_____

_____

_____

_____

_____

_____

_____

_____

_____

_____

_____

_____

_____

_____

_____

_____

Chapter 30 Nouns and Determiners

30a. Nouns

The following paragraph contains count and noncount nouns. Underline the correct form from the choices in parentheses.

        In Canadian supermarkets, new (products, product) and (produce, produces) are constantly being added to the shelves. Children are attracted to new snack foods, and adults are frequently tempted to buy items with (information, informations) about health benefits. To increase consumer (confidence, confidences) in package labelling, the Canadian Food Inspection Agency has announced new (guideline, guidelines) for various claims food manufacturers add to their labels. Products that are advertised as "low (fat, fats)" have to provide (evidence, evidences) on the label and meet new government (standard, standards). For items that appeal to children, the amount of (sugar, sugars) must be clearly indicated. Particularly helpful are the new regulations on serving size because consumers have become very conscious of the amount of (protein, proteins) and (fat, fats) that they eat as well as the number of (calorie, calories).

30a-b. Nouns and Determiners

1.   Write a sentence for each of the words listed below. Some are count nouns, and some are noncount nouns. Use determiners when necessary.

    a.   research

        _____

        _____

    b.   homework

        _____

        _____

    c.   table

        _____

        _____

d.   computer

_____

_____

e.   luggage

_____

_____

f.   system

_____

_____

2.   The words listed below can be count or noncount according to their context. Write appropriate sentences with the determiners that make this distinction clear.

a.   light as a count noun

_____

_____

b.   light as a noncount noun

_____

_____

c.   difficulty as a count noun

_____

_____

d.   difficulty as a noncount noun

_____

_____

e.   crime as a count noun

_____

_____

f.   crime as a noncount noun

_____

_____

g.   game as a count noun

_____

_____

h.   game as a noncount noun

_____

_____

i.   noise as a count noun

_____

_____

j.   noise as a noncount noun

_____

_____

k.   sense as a count noun

_____

_____

l.   sense as a noncount noun

_____

_____

30b. Determiners

1.   In the paragraph below, underline the correct word in parentheses.

   In northern India there is (a, an) conflict between wildlife officials and Gujjar herders of water buffalo. (A, An, The) Indian government wants to turn the area into a national park, to be called the Fajaji National Park, but for the last ten years, local water buffalo herders refuse to move off the land. The Gujjars keep herding their water buffalo, despite warnings that the animals are eating up too (much, many) of the vegetation and that soon

there will be (less, few) areas that have not been destroyed by the herding. Several decades ago, the Gujjars

agreed to migrate every summer to give the forests a chance to grow again, but communities in the areas they

migrated to refused to accept the Gujjars because they needed (a, an, the) land for their own grazing, and they

didn't have (fewer, enough, no) land to share. As a result, the Gujjars now stay in the forest throughout (a, an,

the) year. Government officials keep on warning of (a, an, the) dangers of erosion in the forests where Gujjar

herding has stripped the land. While (some, any, much) environmental groups say that these forest dwellers

have as much right to the land as the animals, other groups support the government's attempt to move the

Gujjars. The continued grazing by water buffalos risks using up the (few, less, little) food sources of elephants

and other animals. Government officials plan to make (a, an) offer to the Gujjars to move them to settlements

on the edge of the forests and to have them feed their animals in stalls. Park officials want to find (a, an)

solution soon because they say that both the park and the Gujjars will suffer if the present situation continues.

2. Write a paragraph of your own correctly using each of the following determiners at least once: a, an, the, some, any, many, few, less, enough. You may want to write about endangered species.

_____

_____

_____

_____

_____

_____

_____

_____

_____

_____

_____

_____

_____

_____

_____

3. In the following paragraph, articles (a, an, the) may or may not be needed before certain nouns. Fill in the blanks with the appropriate article. When no article is needed, leave the blank empty.

   After winding down twenty miles of dirt road in Mtunthama, Malawi, _____ visitors will come upon

the well-kept lawns and gardens of _____Kamuzu Academy, one of _____Africa's most unusual schools. Here,

on four hundred acres of well-trimmed lands is _____school dedicated to classical scholarship. _____school

was founded by President Hastings Kamuzu Banda, the ruler of Malawi since it won its independence from

_____British in 1964. Originally, Dr. Banda studied in _____South Africa, _____United States of America, and

_____Britain, where he acquired _____medical degree and _____love of Latin and Greek, as well as a strong

attraction to the classical emphasis of the elite British schools. When Dr. Banda returned to Malawi, he wanted

to copy _____architecture and curriculum of Eton and other British boarding schools. Some critics in opposition

to Dr. Banda say that _____academy is not appropriate in their country where ordinary schools often do not

have _____textbooks and where more than two-thirds of _____population are illiterate. However, defenders of

the school point out that the school is not elite in choosing its students. Children are accepted without regard to

their family's wealth or position. Each year 35,000 students take _____exam to try to gain entrance to the

school, which accepts about eighty new students _____year. Once accepted, all students are required to take

four years of _____Latin and four years of _____ancient Greek, along with _____English, _____mathematics,

and _____history course about Africa. Most graduates go on to university and then take jobs in _____Malawi

civil service.

30c. Nouns, Pronouns, and Quantifiers

The words listed below can be used as quantifiers to introduce nouns or they can be used as pronouns. For each, write one sentence with the quantifier and one with the pronoun.

a. a little as a quantifier

_____

_____

b. a little as a pronoun

_____

_____

c. few as a quantifier

_____

_____

d. few as a pronoun

_____

_____

e. those as a quantifier

_____

_____

f. those as a pronoun

_____

_____

g. one as a quantifier

_____

_____

h. one as a pronoun

_____

_____

Chapter 31 Verb Patterns

31a. Auxiliary and Main Verbs

1. The following paragraph contains some errors in the verbs. Underline the errors and write your corrections above the words you underlined.

      Wines have been produce in the Champagne district of France for over two thousand years. However, a monk who named Dom Perignon is acknowledge as the father of the delightful celebratory wine known as champagne. He may has brought international fame to the district as early as the 1660s. Dom Perignon, who given his name to one of the priciest brands, did developed and refine his methods in a local monastery. There he used to induced and controlled the second fermentation that might sometimes occurred naturally in the bottle during warm weather. The resulting carbon dioxide which trapped in the bottle will gives "bubbly" its characteristic effervescence. Generations of champagne makers would has refined these techniques until methods were standardize in the 1880s. Now only the product which made and bottled in the Champagne district there is supposed to be call champagne. But wine makers in the Niagara district now producing a variety of sparkling wine called Champagnade that may well outselling the French product in Canada.

2. Use the following verb forms in sentences of your own.

    a.   should + verb

    _____

    _____

    b.   will be + verb

    _____

    _____

    c.   may + verb

    _____

    _____

d. can + verb

_____

_____

e. do + verb

_____

_____

f. may have been + verb

_____

_____

31b. Two-Word (Phrasal) Verbs

Use the following two-word verbs in sentences of your own. If the second word can be separated from the verb in your sentence, a pronoun is included in parentheses.

a. fall behind

_____

_____

b. get out of

_____

_____

c. look like

_____

_____

d. run across

_____

_____

e. call (it) off

_____

_____

f. call (her) up

_____

_____

g. try (it) out

_____

_____

31c. Verbs with -ing and to + Verb Forms

In the following paragraph, underline the correct form of the verb that is called for.

      In Canada, students are expected (to learn, learning) more than just the subject matter they are

beginning (to study, studying). Their teachers urge them (to examine, examining) a subject thoroughly, (to

ask, asking) questions, and even (to disagree, disagreeing) with the opinions of experts if there is good

reason. Educators recommend (to take, taking) such an approach because it helps students (to become,

becoming) better thinkers. Students who are not familiar with the Canadian school system may avoid (to

practise, practising) such critical thinking skills. They may not have been allowed (to question, questioning)

an authority or the written word in their country as a sign of disrespect. Another problem that such students

may encounter in Canada involves (to write, writing) assignments. In Canada students are often asked (to

choose, choosing) topics that argue accepted ideas. Students from other countries often need (to be, being)

encouraged (to express, expressing) opinions without (to apologize, apologizing) because they may have

been forbidden (to discuss, discussing) controversial topics in high school. Students' cultural backgrounds

certainly affect many aspects of academic life, including how they approach the educational experience.

Chapter 32 Idiomatic Usage

32a. Idiomatic Expressions

Write sentences of your own in which you use the following.

a. put up with

_____

_____

b. hold water

_____

_____

c. be on the ball

_____

_____

d. brush up on

_____

_____

e. help out

_____

_____

f. make up (meaning to invent)

_____

_____

g. come across

_____

_____

h. look into (meaning to study or check on something)

_____

_____

i. show up

_____

_____

j. fall behind

_____

_____

32b. Idiomatic Prepositions

1. Write sentences of your own in which you use the following expressions idiomatically.

a. look forward to

_____

_____

b. be tired of

_____

_____

c. apologize for

_____

_____

d. recover from

_____

_____

e. care about

_____

_____

f. rely on

_____

_____

g. be used to (be accustomed to)

_____

_____

h. succeed in

_____

_____

i. insist on

_____

_____

j. fall behind

_____

_____

2. In the following paragraph, underline the correct preposition in parentheses.

Halifax, Nova Scotia, (in, at) the spring of 1851 was a prosperous, diverse city. Halifax was characterized (by, with) a tremendous energy and pursuit (on, of) success that one would expect (for, in) a growing city where the population had just passed 20,000 people. Halifax was somewhat (of, in) a cultural mosaic (with, as) a constantly increasing number of new residents. Many were (in, from) the United States, black loyalists who had fought (for, in) the British in the War of 1812. There were also significant numbers of immigrants (from, in) Germany, Scotland, and Ireland who had been attracted (by, with) the booming fishing market. The 1830s brought (to, in) the previously Protestant Halifax a large number of Irish Catholics whose crops had been devastated (by, from) the potato famine. There were of course large numbers (on, of) French and British descendants who had been living (in, with) conflict there since the 1700s. Inevitably, competition and distrust existed (with, between) the various groups, but gradually these were worked out (at, in) most cases.

3. Write sentences of your own in which you use the following prepositions.

a. on (as a preposition of time)

_____

_____

b. on (as a preposition of place)

_____

_____

c. at (as a preposition of time)

_____

_____

d. at (as a preposition of place)

_____

_____

e. in (as a preposition of time)

_____

_____

f. in (as a preposition of place)

_____

_____

g. of (to show a relationship between a part and the whole)

_____

_____

h. of (to show content)

_____

_____

i.   for (to show purpose)

_____

_____

32c. Idiomatic Sentence Patterns with *There*, *Here*, and *It*

1.   Rewrite the following sentences to begin with "There."

   a.   Many people were complaining about the delays at the airport.

   _____

   _____

   b.   Some kind of thick slime was oozing from the pipe.

   _____

   _____

   c.   A lot of work needs to be done to complete the project.

   _____

   _____

   d.   More than one correct answer exists to this question.

   _____

   _____

2.   Rewrite the following sentences to begin with "It."

   a.   That Eve missed the last bus home was a shame.

   _____

   _____

   b.   To use my new tablet PC is very convenient.

   _____

   _____

c.   Not to be embarrassed when you make a mistake is impossible.

_____

_____

d.   The French exam, not the English exam, is on Tuesday.

_____

_____

32d. Unidiomatic Repetition

In the following sentences, cross out the unnecessarily repeated words.

a.   Students in my class they are looking forward to the upcoming vacation.

b.   My tuition is being paid by an uncle I worked for him after graduating from high school.

c.   Although the accident was minor, yet the driver was still taken to hospital.

d.   My teacher found the book that I left it in the classroom.

e.   The apartment building where I live there has two swimming pools.

f.   My neighbour returned the lawnmower that he had borrowed it.

g.   For many people, they will not walk under a ladder even if they say they are not superstitious.

h.   The pie in the refrigerator it is for tonight's party.

i.   The book drop where library books are returned there is full.

j.   In some parts of Saudi Arabia, ten years may pass there without rain.

32e. Positions for Modifiers

Reorder the following word clusters to create correct sentences, being careful about the placement of the adjectives, adverbs, and nouns. Don't add any words, and be sure to capitalize the first letter of the first word in your sentence.

a.   new   eager   three   students   quickly   the   classroom   entered

_____

_____

b. Japanese   favourite   food   her   is   sushi

_____

_____

c. girls   the   little   were   two   frightened   easily   very

_____

_____

d. almost   experiences   everyone   homesickness   intense   sometimes

_____

_____

e. black   huge   a   menacing   I   suddenly   cloud   spotted

_____

_____

128

PART EIGHT
PUNCTUATION

Chapter 33 End Punctuation

The following paragraph contains some sentences with incorrect use of periods, question marks, exclamation points, and ellipses. Add or change these punctuation marks where they are needed, delete those that are incorrect, and add correct punctuation, if needed. Underline each change you make.

        "Do you see that green area to the left of the river we are flying over"? said the pilot to the passengers as the commercial jet flew over southern Alberta. Continued the pilot, "That's my grandfather's ranch! I often visited there as a kid!" Public-address systems in commercial planes are now being used by pilots to enliven their passengers' flights. Some pilots are opposed to this practice because they see it as a distraction. Says one seasoned veteran, "Our task is to fly the plane, not amuse the passengers". But others disagree. Interesting, informative comments can put nervous passengers more at ease and can shorten a long flight. For those pilots interested in making such public-address announcements, there is now a book put together by an ex-pilot pinpointing more than 1,200 historical and little-known places of interest on a collection of highway maps. The maps are overlaid with the flight paths used by commercial pilots. Are you flying between El Paso, Texas, and Las Vegas, New Mexico. If so, then look for the site of the Berringer Crater, where a meteor hit with such force 22,000 years ago that it killed all animal and plant life within 100 miles! Thousands of these maps have been sold, with more frequent fliers than pilots doing the buying! "We are learning an awful lot about territory we thought we knew"! says one frequent flier who takes her book with her on every flight. Another customer reports, "I bought one for my uncle who hates airplanes, and he now actually enjoys his flights". The book is obviously a success! Who can disagree with an author who predicts, "Soon, there will be such books in the pocket of every seat in every commercial flight?"

Chapter 34 Commas

34a-b. Commas in Series and Lists; Commas with Adjectives

Add commas where needed in the following paragraph to divide items in a series or to separate descriptive adjectives.

When he died in August 2007, Paul MacCready was well known as an award-winning aeronautical engineer the founder of several important scientific companies and an innovative ingenious inventor. He created his first transportation device before graduating from junior high school—a model flying machine that could take off fly and land with little energy power. MacCready was recognized as scientifically gifted from an early precocious age. He trained as a pilot at the end of WWII then completed a bachelor's degree in physics a master's degree in physics and a Ph.D. in aeronautics by the time he was twenty-seven. MacCready became known in the 1970s for a series of fanciful functional aircraft that relied on unusual energy sources like electric power solar power even human power. The three most impressive of MacCready's inventions have ended up in the Smithsonian Institute: the Gossamer Condor the Gossamer Albatross and the solar-powered lightweight car called the Sunraycer. One of his more spectacular creations—a life-sized flying plastic replica of a pterodactyl—was developed for a Smithsonian IMAX production in 1985.

34c. Commas in Compound Sentences

1. The following paragraph contains some compound sentences that need commas. Add commas where they are needed, and underline each comma you have added.

In 1977 the flight of the little airplane, the Gossamer Condor, did not look very impressive but it was indeed a historic flight. With wings of foam, balsa wood, and Mylar, the plane designed by Paul MacCready floated slowly and gracefully over the San Joaquin Valley and covered a mile or so in about eight minutes. What made it so historic was that the pilot was pedalling. The Gossamer Condor was only the first of MacCready's pedal-powered planes and two years later the plane's successor, the Gossamer Albatross, crossed the English Channel. Some people say that MacCready is really the brains behind these inventions but others feel that he receives undue credit for the work that others on the development teams do. However, MacCready was the first to use his observations of how birds fly so his supporters feel that he is the genius who made human-powered flight possible. Other inventors were taking the conventional approach of trying to reduce drag as much as possible because they thought this approach would be the answer. The approaches of other inventors were to streamline their aircraft or they tried to incorporate ways to increase the horsepower. Only MacCready applied the principle of vastly increasing the wing area and used materials to keep the overall weight down. The result was an aircraft that needed only the power output of a good bicyclist and the Gossamer Condor now has a place of honour next to the *Spirit of St. Louis* in the Smithsonian Institute.

2. Write a paragraph with at least four compound sentences that are punctuated correctly with commas. You may want to write about developments in modern transportation methods.

_____

_____

_____

_____

_____

_____

_____

_____

_____

34d. Commas after Introductory Words, Phrases, and Clauses

1. The following paragraph contains some sentences with introductory words, phrases, and clauses that need commas. Add commas where they are needed, and underline each comma you have added.

Having won prizes with his first human-powered plane Paul MacCready went on to build a faster and more powerful pedal-powered plane, the Gossamer Albatross. In less than two years after his first success MacCready's second pedal-powered plane departed from Folkestone, England, in June, 1979, bound for France. Expecting the flight to take about two hours MacCready allotted just enough water for the pilot to drink. The flight team who prepared the plane and assisted the pilot on the ground waited several weeks for the kind of calm weather that was needed. Consequently the pilot took off, expecting to reach France before his endurance and the water gave out. But a head wind blew up soon after the pilot was aloft. An hour and a half later he was only two-thirds of the way to France, and his legs were cramping from all the pedalling. Because everyone was sure they had to give up the attempt the flight team was ready to hook a towline to the craft that would haul it ashore. Tired and about to give up the pilot knew he had to gain altitude to get hooked to the towline. As he climbed he found less wind and was able to press on. Almost three hours later the pilot touched down at Cape Gris-Nez, in France, a minute short of his theoretical exhaustion point. The Gossamer Albatross had crossed the English Channel, powered only by the pilot.

2. Write a paragraph with at least four sentences that have introductory words, phrases, and clauses correctly punctuated with commas. You may want to write about a strenuous sport or competition you have been in.

_____

_____

_____

_____

_____

_____

_____

_____

Commas with Essential and Non-essential Words, Phrases, and Clauses

following paragraph contains some sentences with non-essential words, phrases, and clauses that need
as. Add commas where they are needed, and underline the commas you have added.

After designing human-powered planes, Paul MacCready a prize-winning inventor went on to design a

ed plane. MacCready however realized that solar cells as an energy source for planes do not make

132

any practical sense. But MacCready who had long sympathized with environmental concerns hoped to demonstrate that solar power has an important part in the world's energy future. Those who see solar energy as merely a minor source of energy for the future downplay the importance of such demonstrations. Others think solar power has simply not been adequately developed for practical use. The solar-powered plane that MacCready designed flew from Paris to the coast of England in 1981 cruising at 441 mph at an altitude of 11,000 feet. The plane called the Solar Challenger provided the stepping stone to MacCready's next flying machine the Sunraycer a solar-powered car.

2. Write a paragraph with at least five correctly punctuated sentences that contain essential and non-essential words, phrases, and clauses. You may want to write about the future of solar energy.

_____

_____

_____

_____

_____

_____

_____

_____

_____

34f-h. Comma Conventions; Other Uses for Commas; Inappropriate Commas

The following paragraph contains some sentences with correct commas and some with comma errors. Add commas where they are needed, omit inappropriate commas, and underline each change you make.

The Sunraycer which is a solar-powered lightweight car, was built to compete in the 1987 Race Across Australia. Designed by Paul MacCready the car won the race from Darwin to Adelaide, and is now in the

Smithsonian Institute. With a total weight of 365 pounds the car has a power output of about 1.8 horsepower at noon on a bright day and it gets the electric power equivalent of 500 miles to the gallon. The Sunraycer which presently holds the solar-powered speed record of 48.7 mph averaged a little over 40 mph for much of the race. The car is so light, that when it made turns during testing it often seemed in danger of blowing over. The engineers who worked on the Sunraycer, ended up putting two little ears on the top. "We're not sure why they work" said one engineer "though they seem to help." In some ways the Sunraycer is not a prototype of electric cars for commercial use, because the Sunraycer has bicycle-thin wheels a driver's seat that requires the driver to lie flat, and very weak acceleration. However many of Sunraycer's features were carried over into the electric car developed by General Motors. Like the Sunraycer the GM car uses alternating current, and can therefore get better performance. If electric-powered cars become widely popular in the future Paul MacCready can certainly be credited with having helped save the environment.

34a-h Review of Comma Usage

Commas are used correctly throughout the following paragraph. On the lines below, explain why the commas in each sentence are necessary.

(1) At the turn of the last century, Placentia was a well-established fishing community on the Avalon Peninsula, Newfoundland and Labrador, on the west of the island. (2) This is the community where Thomas Powers and Mollie O'Reilly grew up. (3) He was born in 1888, the son of James and Alice Powers, and Mollie was born to William and Fanny O'Reilly. (4) Both families were respected, hard-working members of the community. (5) Both Thomas and Mollie completed the six grades available at the community school, which meant they were prepared to take their places in the community and to take on the responsibility of marriage and family. (6) Though a few might move to St. John's, the capital, most young men would at that point become fishermen. (7) Having been sweethearts for years, Mollie and Thomas were married on Sunday, January 31, 909, when he was 21 and she was 18. (8) The community at that time saw few big wedding ceremonies. (9) ally the couple informed the minister that they wished to be married at the end of the morning service, and d a simple ceremony with friends and family in the congregation. (10) Thomas and Mollie's wedding, was more memorable than most, as the party that followed lasted for two whole days and nights.

1. _____

   _____

2. _____

   _____

3. _____

   _____

4. _____

   _____

5. _____

   _____

6. _____

   _____

7. _____

   _____

8. _____

   _____

9. _____

   _____

10. _____

   _____

Chapter 35 Semicolons

1. The following paragraph contains some sentences that need semicolons and some sentences with incorrectly used semicolons. Add semicolons or change punctuation marks to semicolons where they are needed, delete those that are incorrect, and add correct punctuation, if needed. Underline each change you make.

Junk mail used to be confined to print on paper, now it is appearing in people's mailboxes on CDs or videodisks. Companies in the direct-mail business are now marketing inexpensive cardboard videodisks that can carry a variety of messages; such as audiovisual advertisements, promotional premiums, and educational or training aids. Some companies are switching to this form of direct-mail advertising because it is relatively cheap, in addition, it presents messages more vividly on screens than print advertising can on paper. Informational videos can be sent to prospective customers, and advertisers feature their product in the video. Says the spokesperson for one cereal company, "We are interested in promoting good nutritional habits;" as might be expected, the balanced diet pictured in the video will include that company's cereal. Printed instructions on merchandise are often confusing, consequently, some manufacturers are also switching to disposable videodisks to deliver information included with the merchandise. The cardboard videodisks are relatively cheap to manufacture and cheap to mail. They are certainly more convenient than the promotional packets sent by companies that have relied on enclosing sample packets of toothpaste, aspirin, or cereal, mail advertisers who send bulky envelopes of coupons, and companies who want to entice customers with big brochures of vacation places, hotels, and tours. The disposable videodisk is certainly growing in popularity as an advertising medium.

2. Write sentences using semicolons in each of the patterns below.

    a. Semicolon in a compound sentence

    _____

    _____

    b. Semicolons in a series

    _____

    _____

Chapter 36 Colons

1. The following paragraph contains some sentences that need colons and some sentences with incorrectly used colons. Add colons or change punctuation marks to colons where they are needed, delete those that are incorrect, and add correct punctuation, if needed. Underline each change you make.

Deciding what to do after graduation is challenging for many university students. For this reason, many Canadian universities have established career centres: where students can research employment opportunities. At the centres, students can do things such as: meet with a career counsellor, practise their interview skills, and revamp their résumés. Here is what one counsellor has to say "When it comes to choosing a profession, many students do not know what opportunities are available to them, and this lack of knowledge is exactly what the career centres seek to remedy." Some of the most important resources at the centres are the personality tests which assess: students' skills and weaknesses and their likes and dislikes. After taking such a test, students can see more clearly what sorts of fields they might excel in. Many career centres also offer: workshops and career fairs. Some students who have visited the campus career centres are thrilled with what they have learned. Just researching what career choices are available has helped many students decide what sort of future they want.

2. Write sentences using colons in each of the patterns below.

a. Colon to announce a single element at the end of a sentence

_____

_____

b. Colon to announce a list at the end of a sentence

_____

_____

c. Colon to announce a long quotation

_____

_____

d.   Colon with quotation marks

_____

_____

Chapter 37 Quotation Marks

1. The following paragraph contains some sentences with correct and incorrect quotation marks. Revise to eliminate errors, adding quotation marks, if needed. Write your changes in above the lines.

"Why am I fatter than my sister-in-law? I eat less, complained a woman being studied by a team of researchers. She explained that she "repeatedly went on diets when her sister-in-law didn't." But the woman continues to weigh more. Researchers are finding out that heredity, in addition to "lifestyle," exerts a strong influence on people's weight. By studying identical and fraternal twins, research teams are finding that brothers and sisters end up with similar body weights whether or not they are raised in different families. In the "Journal of Genetics," Dr. Albert Skinnerd writes, "When the biological parents are fat, there is an 80 percent chance that their children will also be overweight". (234). "Does this mean that my brother and I are doomed to be fat," asked one overweight twin in the study? Since some sets of twins tend to transform extra calories into fat while other sets of twins tend to convert extra calories into muscle, one scientist concluded that "genes do seem to have something to do with the amount you gain when you overeat". Some unsuccessful dieters may be relieved to know that their failed diets aren't a matter of failed "willpower." It is really a matter of metabolism", reports another doctor doing research in this field. But that does not mean that low-fat diets and exercise should be given up. Quit is not a word in my vocabulary", says one constant dieter who manages to maintain a reasonable weight by means of careful eating and plenty of exercise, despite a tendency for extra pounds.

2. Write a paragraph of at least five sentences using at least five sets of quotation marks for direct quotations, minor titles and parts of wholes, words used as words, and other uses of quotation marks. You may want to write about dieting fads by citing sources from online articles.

_____

_____

_____

_____

_____

_____

_____

_____

_____

_____

3. Write a dialogue based on this situation: You and two classmates are discussing an upcoming exam in your literature class. Include at least six separate speeches (two by each speaker, for example) and include titles of a novel and a poem as well as one of a short story, essay, or article that may be covered on the test.

_____

_____

_____

_____

_____

_____

_____

_____

_____

_____

_____

_____

_____

_____

_____

_____

_____

Chapter 38 Apostrophes

1. The following paragraph contains sentences with some apostrophes incorrectly used to show possession, mark contractions, or indicate plurals, as well as some missing apostrophes. Add apostrophes where they are needed (even if they are optional), omit those that are unneeded or incorrect, and underline each change you make.

> In the game of baseball, batting slump's are one of a players worst nightmares. When they are doing well, player's attribute their successes to mysterious minor occurrences around them that then become habits' the players keep up. After a game in which one baseball player who was wearing an old helmet with it's side dented hit two triple's, a home run, and a single, the player continued to wear that helmet for the rest of the season. Warding off evil spirits through superstitions is another thing baseball player's do. One player always wears his favourite T-shirt under his teams jersey. Another wont wear a jersey with any 6s in his players number. Batting coaches spend hours' watching videotapes with slumping players, trying to find whats causing the problem. They examine the players batting stance or swing, but this does'nt always provide useful clues. Some slumps happen when batters begin to worry too much about their misses and about everyone elses successes. But one coach thinks otherwise. He notes that some players' start making adjustments when theyve hit a double and want to hit farther or when a certain unusual pitch connected well with their bats. Players in their '30s complain of a different kind of slump. One bad day, says one over-30 player, may mean he is losing it, that his age has begun to take it's toll. A batters life is'nt as easy as some people think it is.

2. Write at least three sentences that use apostrophes correctly. You may want to write about performance slumps in general or about low periods or slumps in your own life.

_____

_____

_____

_____

_____

Chapter 39 Other Punctuation

1. The following paragraph needs editing of dashes, slashes, parentheses, brackets, and ellipsis points. Add those that are needed, revise any that are not used correctly, and underline all changes that you make.

Which oils are good for us to eat? A study of thirty-nine participants on a reduced-fat diet looked at the

benefits of consuming olive/oil and [or] corn/oil. Which is more beneficial in influencing lipoprotein levels?

This question is important because high-density lipoprotein [HDL] is considered a beneficial form of

cholesterol that helps remove the more dangerous low-density lipoproteins from the body. In a study published

in an article, "Two Healthy Oils for Human Consumption" [*Diet and Health News* 36 (2008): 22-36],

researchers report that the participants first spent twelve weeks on a diet that included olive/oil and then another

twelve weeks on a corn/oil diet. The results—which were widely reported—indicated that neither diet resulted

in lower levels of HDL. Therefore, a diet of olive/oil and (or) corn/oil can safely accompany a reduced-fat diet.

For those who self-select the oils they use in their diet, the choice is probably a matter of taste . . . or cost.

2. Write a paragraph of at least five sentences correctly using one hyphen, one dash, one slash, one ellipsis, one set of parentheses, and one set of brackets. Punctuate everything correctly. You may want to write about healthy eating.

_____

_____

_____

_____

_____

_____

_____

_____

Chapters 33-39 Punctuation Review

Copy a paragraph of eight to twelve sentences from a paper you have recently written or are now working on. Number and correctly punctuate every sentence. On the lines following the paragraph, write the number and briefly justify your choice of each punctuation mark in every sentence.

_____

_____

_____

_____

_____

_____

_____

_____

_____

_____

_____

_____

_____

_____

_____

_____

_____

_____

_____

_____

_____

_____

Explanations:

_____

_____

_____

_____

_____

_____

_____

_____

_____

_____

_____

_____

_____

_____

_____

_____

_____

_____

PART NINE
MECHANICS AND SPELLING

Chapters 40, 41, 42
Capitals, Abbreviations, and Numbers

1. Revise the following paragraph for correct use of capitals and abbreviations, as well as the correct way to write numbers. Underline all changes that you make.

Today, Toronto is one of Canada's largest and most diverse cities. Not many tourists realize that this Modern Capital can also take them on a visit to Canada's past. Visitors interested in the History of Toronto have many hidden away places where they can find relics of the past. They should make a point of visiting Historic Fort York, the location of the Battle of York during the war of eighteen twelve. Fort York is considered the birthplace of modern Toronto. Here, tourists can visit Canada's largest collection of original War of 1812 Buildings, take tours, and watch Musket, Drill, and Music demonstrations. On Victoria Day and Canada Day, the Fort comes to life with nearly 100 costumed actors playing the parts of soldiers, servants, leaders, etc. The fort is almost 3 kilometres long with 12 restored buildings, including the Barracks. Another educational visit would be to the home of William Lyon Mackenzie, one of Canada's most notorious and celebrated figures, whose involvement in the eighteen thirty-seven upper Canada rebellion was made famous in James Reaney's children's book *the Boy with an r in His Hand*. Many tourists do not realize that many of the places mentioned in Reaney's novel are still part of the Toronto landscape, most significantly Mackenzie's Home. This greek-revival row-house was also where Mackenzie, at the time an outspoken newspaperman, put his newspaper to press. Today, visitors can come to its location at 82 Bond St., south of Dundas St., and visit what the home would have been like. It is 2 storeys tall, and the pressroom is built on at the back. Finally, tourists looking to go back in time should visit St. James cathedral, est. 1793. Though the church suffered 2 major fires, parts of the original still endure. This church was used as a Hospital during the war of 1812 and has existed on the same spot since before the town of York became Toronto. Indeed, though Toronto's downtown is incredibly modern, tourists who look carefully can still find reminders of an exciting past.

2. Write a paragraph of at least five sentences correctly using capitals and numbers. Where possible, include appropriate abbreviations of numbers, measurements, and dates. You may want to write about a historic event.

_____

_____

_____

_____

_____

_____

_____

_____

_____

_____

_____

_____

_____

_____

_____

Chapter 43 Underlining/Italics

1. Listed here are titles and words that either need underlines (or italics) or quotation marks. In the right-hand column, write a "U" if the titles or words need an underline (or italics) or "Q" if the titles or words need quotation marks.

   a. Flare (magazine)   <u>   U   </u>

   b. Crash (movie)   _____

   c. The Dirty Thirties (book chapter)   _____

   d. Corner Gas (TV series)   _____

   e. Moby Dick (book)   _____

   f. To His Coy Mistress (short poem)   _____

   g. The Case of the Lost Diamond (TV episode)   _____

   h. The Barber of Seville (opera)   _____

   i. Towards the Last Spike (long poem)   _____

   j. Copenhagen's Museums (magazine article)   _____

   k. Maclean's (news magazine)   _____

   l. Sweet Birdie (song)   _____

   m. Getting Active (pamphlet)   _____

   n. The Economics of Solar Energy (magazine article)   _____

   o. C (letter of the alphabet)   _____

   p. The Colony of Unrequited Dreams (book)   _____

   q. Bluenose (ship)   _____

   r. dejure (Latin phrase)   _____

   s. Music to the Ears (essay)   _____

   t. Ottawa Citizen (newspaper)   _____

2. Write a paragraph of at least five sentences in which you correctly use underlining at least five times. You may want to write about books, magazines, articles, television programs, and movies that you enjoy.

Chapter 44 Spelling

44c. Proofreading

Proofread the following paragraph for spelling errors, typos, and omitted words. Use the dictionary if needed, and underline all the revisions you make. Pay careful attention to punctuation too.

Inventors of gadgets for automobiles havn't always been successful with there inventions. But we can see from some these inventions that people have been looking for ways to make cars more functional, better looking, and more fun to drive, for example, we now have elegent and sophisticated ways to here music in ou cars, but some of the earlier ways to add music to driving seem a bit odd now. In the 1920's, Daniel Young recieved a patent for an organ he invented for use in automobiles. He built organ keyboards that could be accomodated to back of the front seat so that people ridding in the back could play the organ to entertain themselfs. This may have been a good idea, exept for one thing. The roads of that time, unfortunatly, were so bumpy and uneven that the sounds producted by the organ when the car was moving where anythhing but beautiful. Another terriffic idea that didn't make it was Leander Pelton's patent for a car that could be parked by standing it on end. Instead of a back bumper, he build a vertical platform with rolers attached. When parking the Vertical-Park Car, the driver needed to tip the car back onto platform. Than he could just shove the car into any approrpiately sized space. To preform this task, however, was a big dificult as Pelton never quite explained how the car was to be tiped from horzontal to vertical and back down again. A diffrent problem was that Pelton didn't porvide any way to keep gasoline, water, and oil from spilling once the car was up on its parking rollers. But the goverment gave him a patent; he simply couldn't get anyone to manifacture his VerticalPark car. Another invention that never made it was designed by Joseph Grant in 1926—an autombile wash machine. The machin didn't wash cars, but it suppossedly washed clothes. Grant's invention consistted of a tub and paddles that bolted to the car's runing boards. when the tub was filled with water, soap, and drity clothes, the bouncing of the car over rought roads provided all the power and agitatition necessary to clean a load of dirty clothes. For realy dirty load, an extra twenty miles or so of driving was reccommended.

44d. Some Spelling Guidelines

1. **IE/EI:** Using the rules for IE/EI spellings (and the exceptions), underline the correctly spelled words in these sentences.

    a. Does he really (beleive, believe) he will win the lottery?

    b. The soybean (yeild, yield) this year will be high.

    c. She knows how to (seize, sieze) the day.

    d. The (height, hieght) of that tree is unusual.

    e. The company is working hard to establish more (foreign, foriegn) markets.

    f. My (weird, wierd) brother is always trying some crazy new herbal diet.

    g. What is your (field, feild) of study?

    h. Few people carry a (handkercheif, handkerchief) anymore.

    i. He tried to (deceive, decieve) himself into thinking he was able to do that.

    j. I'm so busy that I have no (liesure, leisure) time.

    k. We called off the party when (neither, niether) of the guests of honour could come to it.

    l. During the rainstorm, the (ceiling, cieling) leaked badly.

    m. When is your (neice, niece) coming to visit?

    n. Our new (neighbour, nieghbour) seems like a pleasant person.

    o. The nurse tried to find a (vein, vien).

2. **Doubling Consonants:** Underline the correctly spelled word in these sentences.

    a. I have to be quiet when my uncle is (naping, napping).

    b. It was hard to convince her grandmother to have her (jewelery, jewellery) insured.

    c. Which was the first movie that Paul Newman (starred, stared) in?

    d. As she listened to the music, she kept (tapping, taping) her fingers on the desk.

    e. To whom were you (writting, writing) that long letter last night?

    f. I hope she has (referred, refered) me to a good dentist

    g. Ellen thought her brother looked quite elegant in his (striped, stripped) shirt.

    h. It was a strange (occurrence, occurence) to see the sky lit up like that.

i. I came in at the (begining, beginning) of the movie.

j. They really (benefited, benefitted) from that study session before the exam.

k. My father hates to go (shoping, shopping) when he is on vacation.

l. The advertisement (omitted, omited) any mention of the price.

3. **Doubling Consonants:** Write sentences using the -ed or -ing forms of the words listed here in sentences.

a. shop

_____

_____

b. hope

_____

_____

c. tape

_____

_____

d. star

_____

_____

e. write

_____

_____

f. top

_____

_____

g. slip

_____

_____

h. omit

_____

_____

i. prefer

_____

_____

j. refer

_____

_____

k. benefit

_____

_____

l. occur

_____

_____

4. **Prefixes and Suffixes:** Correctly add the prefixes or suffixes as indicated, and then write a sentence that includes the new word. Consult a dictionary if needed to check on the spelling or the meaning of the word that you have formed.

a. actual + ly

_____

_____

b. ante + cedent

_____

_____

c. anti + biotic

_____

_____

d.   auto + biography

_____

_____

e.   bene + diction

_____

_____

f.   bi + partisan

_____

_____

g.   desire + able

_____

_____

h.   de + value

_____

_____

i.   dis + agree

_____

_____

j.   im + migrate

_____

_____

k.   inter + mission

_____

_____

l.   mis + inform

_____

_____

m. mis + spell

_____

_____

n. notice + able

_____

_____

o. pre + form

_____

_____

p. per + form

_____

_____

q. picnic + ing

_____

_____

r. pro + nounce

_____

_____

s. real + ly

_____

_____

t. true + ly

_____

_____

5. **Y to I:** Correctly add the suffixes given to the words listed here, and then write a sentence using the newly formed word.

a. ready + ed

_____

_____

b. lonely + ness

_____

_____

c. carry + ed

_____

_____

d. carry + ing

_____

_____

e. bounty + ful

_____

_____

f. greasy + ness

_____

_____

g. play + ed

_____

_____

h. employ + ed

_____

_____

i. petty + ness

_____

_____

j. forty + eth

_____

_____

44e. Plurals

For each of the following words write a sentence using the plural form of the word.

1. apology

_____

_____

2. ceremony

_____

_____

3. box

_____

_____

4. city

_____

_____

5. sister-in-law

_____

_____

6. church

_____

_____

7. videocassette recorder

_____

_____

8. radio

_____

_____

9. basis

_____

_____

10. attorney

_____

_____

44f. Sound-Alike Words (Homonyms)

1. Underline the correct word in these sentences.

   a. Everyone came to the concert (accept, except) Tiana.

   b. Does that store (accept, except) personal cheques?

   c. I think the horror movie he saw (affected, effected) his sleep.

   d. The horror movie had no (affect, effect) on him whatsoever.

   e. Her friends were standing (altogether, all together) waiting for her bus to arrive.

   f. (It's, Its) a cool, rainy day today.

   g. I wonder when (it's, its) going to get better.

   h. What is (it's, its', its) temperature?

i.   Last week (passed, past) without incident, fortunately.

j.   She is no bigger (then, than) I am.

k.   Leah stayed until her friend joined her, but (then, than) she left the party.

l.   I hope you don't mind if I sit here for (a while, awhile).

m.   All the speakers (there, their) vowed (there, their) loyalty to the union.

n.   I gave my red sweater (to, too) my sister since I have (to, too) many.

o.   When the bride and groom failed to show, everyone wondered (where, were) they (were, where).

p.   I never know (whose, who's) right in those arguments.

q.   Kristen knows (your, you're) right, but she will never say it to (your, you're) face.

r.   Could you give me some (advice, advise) about (buying, bying) a used car?

s.   That is going to be the (sight, site, cite) for the new shopping mall.

t.   She was (quite, quiet, quit) sure that she had taken her wallet out of her purse.

u.   You have to keep the camera (stationary, stationery) when you take the picture.

v.   Everyone had (all ready, already) left when the music finally began.

w.   I guess it is (alright, all right) to charge that sweater to my mother's account.

x.   Perhaps you can use (anyone, any one) of the golf balls lying there.

2.   Use the following words in sentences. Be sure that you both spell and use them correctly.

a.   accept

_____

_____

b.   except

_____

_____

c. affect

_____

_____

d. effect

_____

_____

e. here

_____

_____

f. hear

_____

_____

g. its

_____

_____

h. it's

_____

_____

i. passed

_____

_____

j. past

_____

_____

k. than

_____

_____

l. then

_____

_____

m. they're

_____

_____

n. their

_____

_____

o. there

_____

_____

p. too

_____

_____

q. to

_____

_____

r. were

_____

_____

s.   we're

_____

_____

t.   where

_____

_____

u.   who's

_____

_____

v.   whose

_____

_____

w.   your

_____

_____

x.   you're

_____

_____

y.   licence

_____

_____

z.   license

_____

_____

aa. site

bb. cite

cc. sight

dd. dessert

ee. desert

Chapter 45 Hyphens

The following paragraph needs to be edited for hyphens. Add those that are missing, revise any that are not used correctly, and underline all changes that you make.

Do you know what your blood-pressure is? A recent study of fifty seven participants says you should. Hyper-tension is on the rise in Canadians from 18-35 years of age. This study by Canadian Health Networks shows the benefits of reducing your blood pressure: risk of heart-attacks is reduced by 25%, stroke by 40% and heart-failure by 50%. Blood pressure numbers are particularly important because most people with high-blood pressure have no symptoms. Just knowing your blood-pressure number can help you take better care of yourself. The article suggests that you can start simply by avoiding products that contain nicotine, like cigarettes, cigars, and tobacco. Exsmokers can see the benefits of lowered blood pressure almost immediately. To stay healthy, Canadian Health Networks recommends that you also limit your alcohol-intake, spend time on things you enjoy and with people you enjoy, manage the stress in your life by avoiding stressful situations, and maintain a healthy weight. For someone who is over-weight, even losing just a few pounds will lead to a significant drop in blood pressure. When you know your blood-pressure-number, you know whether or not you need to change your life-style. If you don't - what will you do?

PART TEN
RESEARCH

Chapter 46 Finding a Topic

46a. Deciding on a Purpose

For each of these topics, determine a purpose you might adopt for writing a research paper about the topic and target an audience for whom you might be writing: volunteering, computers, cultural differences, cloning, politics and the media.

1. Subject: volunteering
    Purpose:

    _____

    Audience:

    _____

2. Subject: computers
    Purpose:

    _____

    Audience:

    _____

3. Subject: cultural differences
    Purpose:

    _____

    Audience:

    _____

4. Subject: cloning
    Purpose:

    _____

    Audience:

    _____

5. Subject: politics and the media
   Purpose:

   _____

   Audience:

   _____

46b. Understanding Why Plagiarism Is Wrong

Write a paragraph explaining your understanding of
- what plagiarism is
- what the consequences of plagiarism are at school or in the workplace
- why plagiarism may occur
- strategies you employ to avoid plagiarism

Include a description of any experience you have had or know about involving plagiarism.

_____

_____

_____

_____

_____

_____

_____

_____

_____

_____

_____

_____

46c-f. Deciding on a Topic, Narrowing the Topic, Formulating a Research Question, and Formulating a Thesis

For each of the general subjects listed below, narrow the subject into a manageable topic for a research paper that would be due two weeks from the date you start. Then formulate a research question about your topic, and formulate a thesis statement that answers your research question.

EXAMPLE

Subject: World War II

Topic: How WWII brought more women into the workforce

Research Question: How did the economic demands of World War II affect women's roles in the workforce?

Thesis Statement: Because World War II created an historic demand for manufacturing while removing almost one-half of the men of working age, women entered the workforce to take up the slack, forever changing societal ideals of women's work.

1. Subject: volunteering
   Topic:

   _____

   _____

   Research Question:

   _____

   _____

   Thesis Statement:

   _____

   _____

2. Subject: computers
   Topic:

   _____

   _____

   Research Question:

   _____

   _____

Thesis Statement:

_____

_____

3. Subject: cultural differences
    Topic:

_____

_____

    Research Question:

_____

_____

    Thesis Statement:

_____

_____

4. Subject: cloning
    Topic:

_____

_____

    Research Question:

_____

_____

    Thesis Statement:

_____

_____

5. Subject: politics and the media
    Topic:

    _____

    _____

    Research Question:

    _____

    _____

    Thesis Statement:

    _____

    _____

Chapter 47 Searching for Information
Chapter 48 Using Web Resources

47a. Choosing Primary and Secondary Sources

Identify each of the research sources listed below as a primary or secondary source for a research paper about Margaret Atwood.

EXAMPLE

"Tricks with Mirrors" (a poem by Margaret Atwood)   <u>primary</u>

1. *The Red Shoes: Margaret Atwood Starting Out* (a book about Margaret Atwood)   _____

2. *The Edible Woman* (a novel by Margaret Atwood)   _____

3. an encyclopedia article about Margaret Atwood   _____

4. a TV documentary about Margaret Atwood   _____

5. *Moving Targets: Writing with Intent* (a book of essays by Margaret Atwood)   _____

6. an internet site about Margaret Atwood maintained by the Margaret Atwood

    Society at Laurentian University   _____

7. an internet site maintained by Margaret Atwood at owtoad.com   _____

47b. Searching the Internet & 48 Using Web Resources

1. Conduct an online search for information on one of the following topics: homelessness, the relation between video games and violence, pro-biotics research, or the effectiveness of political campaign advertising.

    Using correct MLA format, list three sources you found that you might use for a research paper on your chosen topic.

    Topic: _____

    Source 1:

    _____

    _____

    _____

    Source 2:

    _____

    _____

    _____

Source 3:

_____

_____

_____

2. Write a paragraph describing the process you used to find these sources.

_____

_____

_____

_____

_____

_____

_____

_____

_____

_____

_____

_____

47c. Searching Libraries

1. Use the resources available in your school library to locate sources for a research paper on one of the other topics listed in 47b. Using correct MLA format, list three of the sources you found. (See Chapter 53 for a complete listing of MLA formats for various types of sources.)

Topic: _____

Source 1:

_____

_____

_____

Source 2:

_____

_____

_____

Source 3:

_____

_____

_____

2. Write a paragraph describing the process you used to find these sources.

_____

_____

_____

_____

_____

_____

_____

_____

_____

_____

_____

_____

Chapter 49 Evaluating Sources

49b. Evaluating Internet Sources

Choose one of the websites located in the online search in the previous section of this workbook (Ch. 47b & 48). Evaluate that website using the information in Chapter 49, especially the "Checklist for Evaluating Content" on p. 398 in your handbook:

- Who is the author, organization, or sponsor? What are the credentials of this person or organization?
- What evidence is there of the accuracy of the information?
- Is the information current?
- Is there advertising on the site?
- What is the goal of the site?
- How did you access the site? Were there links from reliable sites?
- How good is the coverage of the topic?

_____

_____

_____

_____

_____

_____

_____

_____

_____

_____

_____

49c-d. Evaluating Material for Citation and Evaluating Content

Examine the paragraph in the next exercise (51b) and its bibliographic citation. Evaluate the paragraph for use in an informative paper on world spices.

1. In this space, write your evaluation based on the bibliographic citation (author, timeliness, publisher/producer, audience).

    _____

    _____

    _____

    _____

    _____

    _____

    _____

    _____

    _____

    _____

2. In this space, write your evaluation based on the content (accuracy, comprehensiveness, credibility, fairness, objectivity, relevance, timeliness).

    _____

    _____

    _____

    _____

    _____

    _____

    _____

    _____

    _____

    _____

Chapter 51 Using Sources and Avoiding Plagiarism

51b. Summarizing without Plagiarizing

Write a summary of the following paragraph. Assume that you read the paragraph as part of an article by Frederick Meisnier entitled "Historical Migrations of Foods," in the May 2008 issue of *International Cuisine,* pages 18-27.

> One of the world's most widely used spices is the chili pepper. It gives the characteristic fire to one of India's most well-known foods, curry. In Hungary, chili pepper appears as paprika, adding a crucial bite to the flavor of goulash, and in Italy the use of chili peppers in pepperoni makes the spice a common ingredient in Italian food. The hot flavor of chilies became a staple in various foods of China, Thailand, and other Oriental countries. Five hundred years ago, however, no one in these countries had heard of the chili pepper or even had a word for it, for it was one of the treasures brought back from the New World by Christopher Columbus. When Columbus returned with his new spice, its use soon spread around the globe because it was an interesting addition to the world's spice cabinets and because it traveled well in dried form. There is even evidence of chili peppers being used as a condiment in China within a few decades after it appeared on Spanish tables. The most likely route to the Orient was by sea as the Portuguese engaged in active trading with China, particularly after the founding of their trade colony in Macao. While the Spanish were the first Europeans to encounter the New World peppers, the pepper did not become a distinctive spice in Spanish cooking. It was looked upon more as a curiosity or ornamental than as a fiery way to liven up food. Now, after centuries of use in Central and South America, the chili pepper is finally becoming more popular in North American markets through the increasing interest in Indian, Indonesian, Thai, Vietnamese, and other non-European cuisines.

Write your summary here:

_____

_____

_____

_____

_____

_____

_____

_____

_____

51c. Paraphrasing without Plagiarizing

Paraphrase the first four sentences of the paragraph above.

_____

_____

_____

_____

_____

_____

51d-e. Using Quotation Marks and Using Signal Words and Phrases

Follow the instructions below, using this paragraph from an article by Herbert Benson, M.D., and Julie Corliss, both of Harvard Medical School, and Geoffrey Cowley, *Newsweek*'s health editor. The article is entitled, "Brain Check," and appeared in the September 27, 2004, edition of *Newsweek* on pp. 45-47. This paragraph is on pp. 46-47.

As researchers chart the health effects of hostility and hopelessness, they're also gaining unprecedented insights into the mind's power to heal. The "placebo response" has been widely recognized since the 1950s, when Harvard's Dr. Henry Beecher described the phenomenon. Until recently, most experts dismissed it as a feat of self-deception, in which people who remain sick (or never were) convince themselves they're better. But we're now discovering that expectations can directly alter a disease process. Consider those Parkinson's sufferers who improved with sham surgery. Using PET scans, researchers compared their brains with those of patients who received an active treatment. As expected, the active intervention caused a significant rise in dopamine, the neurotransmitter that people with Parkinson's lack. But the patients who improved on placebo experienced a similar dopamine surge. A related study found that fake analgesics could boost the brain's own pain-fighting mechanisms. In both cases, the placebo response was not an imaginary lessening of symptoms but an objective, measurable change in brain chemistry.

a.	Quote any complete sentence from this paragraph, introducing the quote with a partial sentence of your own that would place the sentence in the context of your paragraph. Use quotation marks and an in-text citation appropriately, and punctuate the entire sentence correctly.

_____

_____

_____

_____

b.	Quote a sentence from this paragraph, leaving out several words in the middle of the sentence. Introduce the sentence appropriately, include an in-text citation, and punctuate correctly.

_____

_____

_____

c.	Quote a sentence that includes a quotation. Introduce the sentence appropriately, include an in-text citation, and punctuate correctly.

_____

_____

_____

_____

d.	Paraphrase the last two sentences of the paragraph, quoting at least three words in sequence from one of those sentences. Introduce the sentence appropriately, include an in-text citation, and punctuate correctly.

_____

_____

_____

_____

PART ELEVEN
MLA DOCUMENTATION

Chapter 53 Documenting in MLA Style

1. Included below is a paragraph about women hikers. Following the paragraph are some sentences with information that can be added to the paragraph either as direct quotations or as information written in your own words whose source must be cited. Rewrite the paragraph so that you add at least two direct quotations and one paraphrase. Be sure to integrate the quotations and paraphrase into the paragraph, cite the sources in the paragraph, and include a list of Works Cited (in MLA format) at the end of the paragraph.

> Among the other worlds of outdoor sports and recreation that women were entering before the turn of the century was hiking. Annie Smith Peck joined the list of great alpinists when she reached the peak of the Matterhorn in 1895. She was the first woman to wear pants for climbing, even though at that time women all wore floor-length skirts. Peck continued her climbing and hiking until she was seventy-five years old, including the historic first ascent of Mount Huascaran in Peru, a climb that went above 22,000 feet. In 1901, six years after Peck's assault on the Matterhorn, women joined the first Sierra Club hike. Despite Peck's famous knickerbocker pants, the Sierra Club's stated policy was that women wear skirts which could be no shorter than halfway from knee to ankle. Female hikers in great climbs became increasingly common, though not always as colorful as the famous Grandma Gatewood (Emma Gatewood), the first woman to hike the entire Appalachian Trail in one continuous stretch, in 1955. At the age of sixty-seven she hiked in sneakers and slept on a plastic shower curtain. Grandma Gatewood went on to hike the great Appalachian Trail two more times in her career.

Material to add to your version of the paragraph:

a. The historian Iris Koach, in a book entitled *Women in Sports* (published in Toronto in 2002 by Littleton Publishing), wrote the following sentence, which appears on page 81:

> "Annie Smith Peck, a product of genteel Victorian wealth and exclusive private schooling, became intrigued with the idea of laying aside her scholarly efforts in order to scale the Matterhorn."

b. On page 172, Koach mentions Emma Gatewood:

> "With little publicity and less interest in commercial support for her efforts, Emma Gatewood continued to set hiking records until well into her eighties. She was an inspiration for women

who saw themselves as too frail or inexperienced to hike on their own or without the support of a group of men."

c.   The following sentence appears on page 45 of *Hiking Canadian* by Erwin Moser (published in 2008 by Missing Link Press in Toronto):

"By the 1950s, equipment for hiking filled specialty catalogues and was taking over more and more space in sporting goods stores. The selection of hiking boots, tents, backpacks, cooking utensils, and other gear had become a complicated science."

Your version of the original paragraph with the material added:

_____

_____

_____

_____

_____

_____

_____

_____

_____

_____

_____

_____

_____

_____

Your Works Cited page for your version of the paragraph you wrote in the last exercise:

_____

_____

_____

_____

_____

_____

_____

_____

2. Listed here are a variety of sources that were used to write a paper. Using every entry listed, prepare a Works Cited page according to MLA style.

    a. A book by Dennis Raphael entitled *Poverty and Policy in Canada: Implications for Health and Quality of Life* published in Toronto by Canadian Scholars Press in 2007. The paper cited information from pages 12 to 22 of this book.

    b. A book by Norma Polovitz Nickerson and Paula Kerr entitled *Snapshots: An Introduction to Tourism* published in Toronto by Pearson Prentice Hall in 2007. The paper cited information from pages 262-263.

    c. A book entitled *Creating Postwar Canada: Community, Diversity, and Dissent, 1945-75* edited by Robert Allen Rutherdale and Magdalena Fahrni and published in Vancouver by UBC Press in 2008. The paper cited information from page 74.

    d. A poem by John Newlove entitled "Ride Off Any Horizon" appearing in the anthology entitled *15 Canadian Poets x 3*, 4th edition, edited by Gary Geddes and published in Don Mills by Oxford University Press in 2001. The poem is on pages 229 to 232.

    e. A magazine article by Valerie Jamieson entitled "Atomic Logic" appearing on pages 44-47 of the February 9, 2008, edition of *New Scientist* magazine.

    f. An interview with Marla Shapiro on the television program *Canada A.M.,* produced by CTV and aired on channel CKCO out of Kitchener on February 7, 2008.

    g. A citation from William Shakespeare's *Hamlet*, taken from a collection of Shakespeare's work on CD-ROM published by CMCReSearch in 1989. The CD-ROM program does not list a place of publication.

    h. Material from an online information service, Dialog, from file 102, item 0346142. The material came from an article by Walter S. Baer entitled "Telecommunications Technology in the 1990s," published in the June 1994 edition of *Computer Science* magazine. The article began on page 152 and continued on various pages throughout the magazine.

Your Works Cited page for the sources listed in this exercise:

_____

_____

_____

_____

_____

_____

_____

_____

_____

_____

_____

_____

_____

_____

_____

_____

_____

_____

3. Write an informative paragraph on chili peppers by using the information in the exercise in Chapter 51b, as well as information from **two** other sources you have found through research. Incorporate information by paraphrasing, summarizing, and quoting as appropriate from all three sources and provide parenthetical citations in MLA format. List the three sources at the end of your paragraph using MLA format for references.

_____

_____

_____

_____

_____

_____

_____

_____

_____

_____

_____

_____

_____

_____

_____

_____

_____

_____

Works Cited

_____

_____

_____

_____

_____

_____

_____

_____

_____

_____

_____

PART TWELVE
APA, CM, CSE, AND COS DOCUMENTATION

Chapter 54 Documenting in APA Style

1. Included here is the same paragraph about women hikers as used in the first exercise for Chapter 53. Following the paragraph are some sentences with information that can be added to the paragraph either as direct quotations or as information written in your own words. Rewrite the paragraph so that you add at least two direct quotations and one paraphrase. Be sure to integrate the quotations and the paraphrase into the paragraph, cite the sources in the paragraph, and include a list of the works you referenced (in APA format) at the end of the paragraph.

   Among the other worlds of outdoor sports and recreation that women were entering before the turn of the century was hiking. Annie Smith Peck joined the list of great alpinists when she reached the peak of the Matterhorn in 1895. She was the first woman to wear pants for climbing, even though at that time women all wore floor-length skirts. Peck continued her climbing and hiking until she was seventy-five years old, including the historic first ascent of Mount Huascaran in Peru, a climb that went above 22,000 feet. In 1901, six years after Peck's assault on the Matterhorn, women joined the first Sierra Club hike. Despite Peck's famous knickerbocker pants, the Sierra Club's stated policy was that women wear skirts which could be no shorter than halfway from knee to ankle. Female hikers in great climbs became increasingly common, though not always as colorful as the famous Grandma Gatewood (Emma Gatewood), the first woman to hike the entire Appalachian Trail in one continuous stretch, in 1955. At the age of sixty-seven she hiked in sneakers and slept on a plastic shower curtain. Grandma Gatewood went on to hike the great Appalachian Trail two more times in her career.

Material to add to your version of the paragraph:

a. The historian Iris Koach, in a book entitled *Women in Sports* (published in Toronto in 2002 by Littleton Publishing), wrote the following sentence, which appears on page 81:

> "Annie Smith Peck, a product of genteel Victorian wealth and exclusive private schooling, became intrigued with the idea of laying aside her scholarly efforts in order to scale the Matterhorn."

b. On page 172, Koach mentions Emma Gatewood:

"With little publicity and less interest in commercial support for her efforts, Emma Gatewood continued to set hiking records until well into her eighties. She was an inspiration for women who saw themselves as too frail or inexperienced to hike on their own or without the support of a group of men."

c. The following sentence appears on page 45 of *Hiking Canadian* by Erwin Moser (published in 2008 by Missing Link Press in Toronto):

"By the 1950s, equipment for hiking filled specialty catalogues and was taking over more and more space in sporting goods stores. The selection of hiking boots, tents, backpacks, cooking utensils, and other gear had become a complicated science."

Your version of the original paragraph with the material added:

_____

_____

_____

_____

_____

_____

_____

_____

_____

_____

_____

_____

_____

_____

_____

_____

_____

Your References page for your version of the paragraph you wrote in the last exercise:

_____

_____

_____

_____

_____

_____

_____

_____

2. Listed here are a variety of sources that were used to write a paper. Using every entry listed, prepare a References page according to APA style.

    a. A book by Dennis Raphael entitled *Poverty and Policy in Canada: Implications for Health and Quality of Life* published in Toronto by Canadian Scholars Press in 2007. The paper cited information from pages 12 to 22 of this book.

    b. A book by Norma Polovitz Nickerson and Paula Kerr entitled *Snapshots: An Introduction to Tourism* published in Toronto by Pearson Prentice Hall in 2007. The paper cited information from pages 262-263.

    c. A book entitled, *Creating Postwar Canada: Community, Diversity, and Dissent, 1945-75,* edited by Robert Allen Rutherdale and Magdalena Fahrni and published in Vancouver by UBC Press in 2008. The paper cited information from page 74.

    d. An article entitled "Canadians on the Move" appearing in the fact book entitled *Canadian Global Almanac* edited by Susan Girvan and published in Toronto by Macmillan Canada in 2000. The paper cited information from page 67.

    e. A magazine article by Valerie Jamieson entitled "Atomic Logic" appearing on pages 44-47 of the February 9, 2008 edition of *New Scientist* magazine.

f.   An interview with Marla Shapiro on the television program *Canada A.M.,* produced by CTV and aired on channel CKCO out of Kitchener on February 7, 2008.

g.   A citation from William Shakespeare's *Hamlet,* taken from a collection of Shakespeare's work on CD-ROM published by CMCReSearch in 2008. The CD-ROM program does not list a place of publication.

h.   Material from an online information service, Dialog, from file 102, item 0346142. The material came from an article by Walter S. Baer entitled "Telecommunications Technology in the 1990s," published in the June 1994 edition of *Computer Science* magazine. The article began on page 152 and continued on various pages throughout the magazine.

Your Reference page for the sources listed in this exercise:

_____

_____

_____

_____

_____

_____

_____

_____

_____

_____

_____

_____

_____

_____

3. Write an informative paragraph on what studies have shown about the effect of the mind-body connection on health by using the information in the paragraph in the exercise for Chapter 51d-e, as well as information from **two** other sources you have found through research. Incorporate information by paraphrasing, summarizing, and quoting as appropriate from all three sources and provide parenthetical citations in APA format. List the three sources at the end of your paragraph using APA format for references.

_____

_____

_____

_____

_____

_____

_____

_____

_____

_____

_____

_____

_____

_____

_____

_____

_____

_____

References

_____

_____

_____

_____

_____

_____

_____

_____

_____

_____

_____

Chapter 55 Documenting in Other Styles

Choose the letter for the preferred documentation style for source citations on each of these topics:

	Topics			**Style for Citations**
1.	War-time journalism	_____	A.	*Chicago Manual of Style*
2.	Astronomical calculations	_____	B.	*The CSE Manual* (Council of Science Editors)
3.	Journal of Medieval History	_____	C.	*The Canadian Press Stylebook*
4.	Biological control of garden pests	_____	D.	*The AMS Author Handbook*
5.	Geometrical theories	_____	E.	*AIP Style Manual*

ANSWER KEY

In some cases, responses to exercises will vary, in particular when original sentences and paragraphs are to be written in response to the exercises. Other exercises require specific revision, but the method of revision may vary. In those cases, one example of a possible revision is provided in this Answer Key. Other exercises can only be revised or responded to in one specific way, and in those cases, the answers are provided here.

PART TWO

Chapter 3 Paragraphs

3a. Unity
Responses will vary but should mention that the sentence about the weather in Tibet should be deleted for the sake of unity.

3b. Coherence
Responses will vary but should mention that although the paragraph is well written, it would benefit from added transition between sentences.

3c. Development
Responses will vary but should mention that the inadequate development can be repaired by adding examples of what critics have said.

Chapter 4 Argument

4d. Logical Fallacies
3. a.   either…or
    b.   ad hominem (or non sequitur)
    c.   bandwagon
    d.   circular reasoning
    e.   non sequitur

PART THREE

Chapter 6 Document Design

6a. Principles of Document Design
The restaurant guide lists ethnic restaurants two ways:
1. By ethnicity
    * Chinese restaurants
    * Italian restaurants
    * Middle Eastern restaurants
    * Mexican restaurants
2. By neighbourhood

6c. Webpage Design

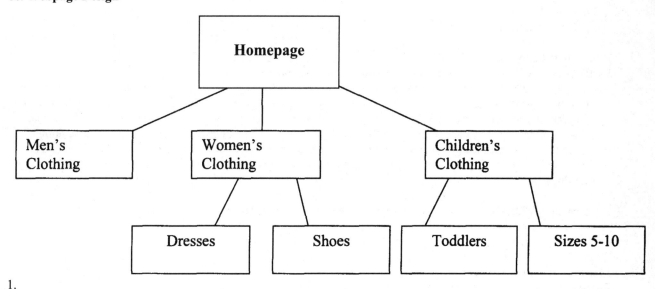

1.

6d. Presentation Format
1. APA
2. MLA
3. APA
4. MLA
5. MLA
6. APA
7. APA
8. APA

Chapter 9 Writing about Literature

9d. Conventions in Writing about Literature
1. past tense
2. present tense
3. present tense
4. past tense

PART FOUR

Chapter 11 Precise Words

11a. Denotation and Connotation
1. Responses will vary, but possible responses are provided here.
    a. famous
    b. pushy
    c. conservative
    d. compulsive
    e. janitor
    f. used car
    g. soil
    h. smell
    i. finicky
    j. below average

11b. General and Specific Words
1. Responses will vary, but one possible revision is provided here.

    People like driving up for fast food, and now so do their spaniels and collies. A new fast-food industry has begun for drive-in dog food, and the menu is entirely for dogs. These new businesses offer treats to dogs with dog biscuits shaped to resemble the kind of fast food people have. The dog biscuits are made from foods that help keep dogs healthy. The biscuits are flavoured differently so that dogs don't get tired of the same thing. Customers love the idea of going to a doggy drive-in after picking up their own fast food. So far the menu has been limited to dog biscuits, but inventive dog food chefs will come up with new ideas for better food products for dogs.

2. General Words: soup, ingredients, leftovers, dried herbs, vegetable-flavoured waters
    Specific Words: Grandmaman, stock pot, Sunday's dinner, Tuesday's lunch, chunks of chicken, meatball, carrots, broccoli, asparagus, plastic margarine tubs, fridge, soup pot

11c. Concrete and Abstract Words
Responses will vary, but one possible revision is provided here.

When hikers reach a stream, they often decide to cross where the dirt trail slopes down to the water. But this may not be the best place at which to cross. Water usually moves most swiftly at the narrowest part of the stream. So, hikers should instead look for another spot where the stream widens. Here the current often slows down and may be easier to walk through. When hikers are carrying a backpack, they should loosen the shoulder straps and hip belt before wading in so that they can toss off the pack if they stumble or lose their balance. Some hikers find that if they suddenly hit a depression in the streambed, the weight of the backpack can toss them off balance. Another aid to crossing a stream is a good hiking stick. It can serve as another leg, offering better balance when there are slippery rocks underfoot. It is helpful to remove unneeded sweaters, heavy pants, or boots before crossing a stream with a swift current because the water can drag against waterlogged vests and jeans. The hiker should also take each step slowly and deliberately. The forward foot should be planted firmly before the rear foot is moved. The careful hiker never hurries across a stream.

Chapter 12 Appropriate Words

12a-b. Standard English, Colloquialisms, Slang, and Regionalisms
1. I'm certainly not planning to take those people to the final.
2. Jason watched a science fiction movie and then fell asleep on the sofa.
3. A soft drink now costs at least two dollars.
4. I'm not worried about the English exam, but I'm quite nervous about the history exam.
5. My friends were amazed when they saw that I had had my tongue pierced.

12c. Levels of Formality

Responses will vary, but one possible revision is provided here.

   People interested in tracing their heritage now have new possibilities. In earlier times, they were forced to rely on old photographs or recollections of their grandparents. Those methods were not foolproof, however. Photographs can be deceiving, and older people forget dates. Now scientists have developed a promising new approach that is gaining popularity because of its accuracy. All anyone needs to do is secure a sample of his or her DNA material, which conveys considerable information about the person and the person's ancestors. With a simple swab from the inside of the cheek, scientists can trace anyone's ancestors, even all the way to Africa, where they think human life began. Amazingly, this DNA "fingerprinting," inherent in everyone's genes, is waiting to be discovered. The only obstacle is that women can trace information only from their mothers because they lack a Y chromosome that men possess. It is, therefore, the man in a family who must trace the male side through his DNA.

12d. Jargon and Technical Language

1.   The doctor admitted that over-the-counter cold remedies would counteract his prescription for my upset stomach.
2.   Our pottery teacher has a low salary and few benefits.
3.   Our supervisor has asked us to re-examine the situation and recommend solutions.
4.   The model suggests that the more serious a student is, the higher the marks.
5.   A team of paleontologists is evaluating the iron content of mesolithic rocks.

12e. Pretentious Language

1.   a.   I determined that my speech to the students required considerable revision.
     b.   The gravity of the situation left her speechless.
     c.   My co-worker, Nathan, is a character.
     d.   The snow-covered evergreens sparkled in the early morning sunshine.
     e.   Everyone was struck by the clarity of the speaker's comments.

2.   Responses will vary, but one possible revision is provided here.

   As the twenty-first century progresses, colleges and universities are trying to appeal to diverse students and provide wider access by offering classes in various formats. Students may study in traditional classrooms or complete an entire degree online without ever coming to a campus. Online classes are conducted exclusively through the internet. If you are considering online education, you should be aware of the personal characteristics necessary for success in this environment. You must be self-disciplined and not inclined to procrastinate, and you must have excellent reading skills. Contrary to what many students think, online classes are not easier, but require much more time and concentrated effort than traditional classes. If you earn a degree online, however, you will have excellent computer skills, as well as knowledge of the subject matter.

12g-h. Offensive Language and Inclusive Language

Responses will vary, but one possible revision is provided here.

   In many suburban housing developments built during recent decades there are homeowners associations that enforce housing codes on all the homeowners. The average owners in such a suburb may think that they are free to paint their houses whatever colour they like or park any kind of car in their driveways, but that is not the case. Homeowners associations often have a lawyer who spends his or her days enforcing the laws enacted by these associations. The laws see to it that all the members abide by the group's standards of good taste. No plastic flamingos are allowed on the lawn, and all house painters who work in the suburb know that they cannot use certain colours for house trim, such as bright pink or a gaudy yellow, because they have to follow community guidelines. When houses are built in new developments, there are usually restrictive covenants that force buyers to join the association, whether they like it or not. Even when people challenge the laws, they usually lose as the covenants are legally binding. It all starts with the builder because when builders build, they want to make certain that the land value for the community stays high so that they can continue to sell their houses at a good price. The builder often starts off as the chairperson of the homeowners association so that he or she can guide the formation of the rules and regulations. In one exclusive community in the States there are even regulations for local government and civil servants, including dress codes for police officers, taxi drivers, and mail carriers. The only challenges that have gotten through the courts are those that show some regulation discriminates on the basis of race, religion, sex, or other characteristics of the homeowner.

PART FIVE

Chapter 13 Sentence Variety

1. 1. c
    2. c
    3. e
    4. c
    5. b
    6. e
    7. c
    8. a
    9. a
    10. e
    11. d

2. Responses will vary, but one possible revision is provided here.

    Animal rights activists, known primarily for their campaigns against fur coats and the use of animals in laboratories, are also campaigning against the Calgary Stampede, the world's largest rodeo. In public statements, protestors say that rodeo animals are being mistreated, citing in support the numerous deaths of horses and cattle during the Stampede. Rodeo cowboys dispute the claims of animal rights activists that rodeo horses buck because they are in pain. Where the activists call even accidental death of these horses abuse, Stampede organizers point out that deaths are rare and that the owners make great effort to take care of their horses. Treated like star athletes and kept well fed and comfortable, the animals enjoy performing. In argument, animal rights activists condemn calf roping, pointing to the injuries of several calves in the past years. It is true that roping breaks calves' necks and can also snap vertebrae and legs, yet eliminating calf roping would mean an end to the rodeo part of the Stampede. Stampede enthusiasts argue that this would end a long-standing tradition and that most animals are not harmed. Animal rights activists counter with the statement that any tradition which harms animals is barbaric. Organizers point out that there are thorough investigations whenever any animal is injured. They invite activists to see for themselves by joining the over one million spectators at the Calgary Stampede each year.

5. Responses will vary, but one possible revision is provided here.

    Gardening can be a worthwhile activity because the gardener can produce food for her family, as well as helping to save the environment and prevent the overuse of landfills. One way to do this is by mulching, which is actually recycling. The gardener can recycle clippings when she mows the lawn in the summer and leaves when she rakes in the fall, along with scraps from the kitchen all year long. Usually the clippings, leaves, and scraps are gathered in large plastic bags and taken to the landfills. To use these items as organic mulch, the gardener should collect them in a corner of the garden and mix them all together. Later, she can spread the mulch on the garden to provide nutrients which will cause the soil to produce bigger and better vegetables, thus providing her with many benefits.

Chapter 14 Comma Splices and Fused Sentences

Responses will vary, but one possible revision is provided here.

    Where Canadians in the '60s were known as a nation of savers, nowadays we seem to be encouraged to spend as much as possible as quickly as possible. This attitude is expressed on television; advertising also plays on this appeal. Many see a relationship between these current attitudes and gambling on lotteries. It is easy to understand why more and more people are handing their money over to chance, fate, and luck if what they are looking for is instant gratification. Statistics show this attitude is growing: in the late '80s, lotteries grew an average of 17.5 percent annually—roughly as fast as the computer industry. High-tech advertising for the lotteries takes attention away from the fact that a player has virtually no chance of winning. Advertisements, instead, focus on the fantasy of what it would be like to win. Surveys conducted by lotteries show that few players have a clear understanding of how dismal their odds of winning really are. A player has a better chance of being struck by lightning than of winning a lottery.

Chapter 15 Sentence Fragments

1. 1. complete sentence
    2. complete sentence
    3. fragment
    4. complete sentence
    5. fragment
    6. complete sentence
    7. fragment
    8. complete sentence
    9. complete sentence
    10. fragment
    11. complete sentence

Chapter 16 Coordination and Subordination

1. Responses will vary, but one possible revision is provided here.

    We are movie addicts. Because over 75 percent of all households now have DVD players, hotels now make their guests feel at home by providing DVD players for watching movies. Some of the largest hotel chains have added DVD players in every room and arranged for the rental of DVDs from shops in the hotel. In these shops, which have a good selection of recent movies, hotel guests can show their room card and can rent a movie at a reasonable rate. Other hotels don't want to bother with stores in the lobby, and they are exploring a different option. In their lobbies, they are adding automated video dispensing machines that hold hundreds of titles and have new releases as well as standard favourites. One hotel chain, which has a lot of large business conventions, has investigated another approach. It is offering to distribute to guests DVDs that the corporation holding the convention wants its participants to see. Corporations like this because the DVDs can convey some of the key ideas being presented at the convention. DVD players in hotel rooms may soon be standard equipment, just as television sets were added years ago when we became addicted to television and first started expecting to watch television in our hotel rooms.

2. a. Although junk food is usually low in nutritional value and high in price, people buy a lot of it anyway.
    b. Children with disabilities deserve the special attention they can get from schools—not just from the teachers who are specially trained to work with them but also from their peers.
    c. Because it has been a terribly cold winter, people have been feeding the ducks that have had trouble finding food.

Chapter 17 Parallel Constructions

1. Recently, two pilots, <u>one in a 175-seat commercial airliner</u> and <u>the other one in a small, twin-engine corporate jet</u>, were barrelling toward each other. On the instrument panel of the commercial jet, <u>a small air traffic screen flashed a yellow circle</u> and <u>a voice announced, "Traffic."</u> As the yellow circle approached the centre of the screen, it changed to a red square. The voice said loudly, "Climb, <u>climb."</u> <u>As he noticed the red square</u> and <u>as he pulled up</u>, the pilot saw the other craft fly past several hundred feet below. The voice that called out the warning was <u>not the copilot</u> but <u>the latest audiovisual aid to arrive in cockpits of planes</u>, a traffic alert and collision avoidance system, called ACAS (Airborne Collision Avoidance System). Transport Canada <u>modified</u> the Canadian Aviation Regulations in 2007 and <u>issued</u> an order requiring <u>that the ACAS system be mandatory for all newly manufactured airplanes in Canada</u> and <u>that all commercial airplanes meet the standards within two years</u>. The system works by <u>computing the distance between planes</u>, <u>warning planes when they get within six miles of each other</u>, and then deciding which plane should climb and which should descend to avoid a collision.

Chapter 18 Sentence Clarity

1. Responses will vary, but one possible revision is provided here.

     A new approach to using computers may be to jot handwritten notes onto an electronic pad. This is done by a special pen that projects a narrow light beam onto the pad. For computer users who have had to rely on entering data into a computer by means of a keyboard, it is a major step forward in using computers. Typing is more distracting than writing for many people who are not skilled typists but who use computers frequently. For the last twenty-five years, the goal of computer developers has been to rid the computer of keyboards, but more development in the field of character recognition is needed. One way to eliminate the keyboard is to teach computers to read through optical character recognition. Another way is to recognize the human voice instead of typed data. But speech recognition is not advancing as rapidly as some computer developers would like. It is not likely that we will soon see computers we can converse with because we have no technology that is so advanced. More promising is the ability of the computer to scan images. Already character recognition machines scan pages of printed material. Computer developers are also considering electronic gloves that could be used by people to point to areas of the screen. There is no limit to what will be coming next in computer development. The result of doing away with the keyboard will be to save time and to eliminate all the typographical errors.

Chapter 19 Transitions

1. Responses will vary, but one possible revision is provided here.

     My father really needs help because he is a workaholic. In other words, he works nearly fourteen hours a day. Doctors have told him not only that it is bad for his health but that it is affecting his family too. In fact, he has worried my mother to no end. Of course, my family has tried to help him, but he has not acknowledged the problem. My dad has a commitment to his company that is hard to imagine. For example, he sneaks out of the house before anyone is awake, and he gets home after most of us have finished dinner and are getting ready for bed. Then he works at home with his computer connected to the one at his office. It's bad enough that his work can call him at home because he has a pager and a cell phone. Things may even be getting worse, for Dad has now accepted a promotion to regional director.

Chapter 20 Sentence Economy

1. Responses will vary, but one possible revision is provided here.

     Telling time is vital to us all, even though the concept of time has changed. Time is the essential measure against which other important measurements are made. For example, we measure our bodies' heart rates and the speed of our cars in terms of time. We organize our days and nights into segments of time, just as people have always measured time by counting sunrises and sunsets or observing the movements of the moon and the sun. For centuries, speculation about the nature of time was mostly a philosophical discussion of how people perceive time and experience its passage. But in twentieth-century science, since Albert Einstein, physicists have come to realize that time is a dimension of the physical universe. Time is a measure of motion in space, not some philosophical or theoretical unknown that exists in people's minds. Einstein also showed that time is not absolute or unique. People used to think that any event measured in time would be seen to take the same amount of time. That is, two accurate clocks in working order would agree on the time interval between two events. But the discovery that the speed of light appears the same to every observer, no matter how he or she is moving, led to the theory of relativity. Now time is seen to be relative to the observer who measures it. Each observer can have his or her measure of time as recorded by the clock he or she carries. Clocks carried by different observers do not necessarily have to agree. This is a very different view of time from the older one. However, even with this notion that time is not absolute, we still use time as a means of measurement.

2. Responses will vary, but one possible revision is provided here.

     Many people today are so devoted to their pets, particularly their dogs, that they think they cannot live without them. Whether the pet is a gigantic, wise-looking mastiff or a yappy Chihuahua, all owners consider their pets indispensable. Rational pet owners are seldom found. Many dress their pets in expensive clothes they buy on the Internet or in fancy pet stores. They may buy expensive pet beds or send their pets to doggie daycare when they go to work. Many would take their pets to work with them if it were allowed. People who don't own pets may think their pet-owning friends crazy to spend so much money, time, and energy on their pets, but true pet lovers feel more at ease with their animal friends and are willing to do whatever seems necessary to keep them happy.

Chapter 21 Consistency (Avoiding Shifts)

1. Responses will vary, but one possible revision is provided here.

    High school formals used to be dances where students dressed up in suits and dresses and celebrated their coming graduation, but now they have to spend big bucks for a tuxedo or elegant formal dress. Graduation has become big business as formalwear shops and limousine services offer their services in advertising campaigns. Tuxedo rental shops across the country report that graduation dances, not weddings, account for the major portion of their business. One local shop owner said that he used to look forward to summer as his busy season because of weddings but that he now makes more money in the spring because of graduations. The typical expenses now include the tuxedo rental, tickets, corsage, dinner, and limousine rental. High school graduates can easily spend $300 on the dance, and that is just for the basics. Graduates can spend additional funds for the latest fashions in tuxes, and they can buy photos for $50 or more. Even when the event is over, there are other expenses. Some graduates go away for the whole weekend, often to a resort hotel. So there are additional costs for a hotel, and if parents are along as chaperones, it is necessary to add in the cost of their rooms and meals too. High school graduates insist that this is all necessary as a rite of passage, but the parents, who often have to contribute most of the funds, do not appreciate the expense. Now even public school students have begun to imitate their elders. Grade eight graduates now take part in expensive formal celebrations as well.

Chapter 22 Subject-Verb Agreement

1. Beloved of Canadian and international readers is one of the funny page's most successful cartoonists, Lynn Johnston. Currently featured in over 2000 papers in Canada and abroad, Johnston's "For Better or For Worse" was first published in 1979. Everyday family issues like doing the dishes and trouble with school are turned into often funny, often heart-warming jokes by Johnston. Johnston planned to retire in the fall of 2006, but after being asked to reconsider by her publisher, she has made "For Better or For Worse" live on as a "hybrid-comic." The idea of the hybrid-comic is to combine new material with old comic strips, which are flashbacks to a different time in the life of the characters. If it is successful, Johnston may continue for years to come: her fans will get to follow the adventures of the Pattersons and their friends as they live everyday struggles. When will Johnston retire? It is too soon to know for sure, but for now her hybrid comic is still keeping millions entertained.

2. is
    weighs
    finds
    sell
    is
    want
    depends
    is
    strike
    do
    are
    are
    is

3. Sentences will vary but the verb forms should be as follows:
    a. Singular

b. Plural
c. Plural
d. Plural
e. Plural
f. Plural
g. Singular
h. Singular
i. Singular
j. Plural
k. Singular
l. Singular or plural depending upon how committee is used
m. Singular
n. Plural
o. Singular
p. Singular
q. Plural
r. Singular
s. Plural
t. Singular
u. Plural
v. Singular
w. Plural

Chapter 23 Mixed Constructions

23a. Faulty Predication
1. With the present concern for the environment, some companies are trying to increase their sales by advertising their products as environmentally safe. The makers of some plastic trash bags, for example, are claiming that their plastic is degradable. The reason for the claim is that there are additives that cause the product to break down after prolonged exposure to sunlight. Biodegradability, they assert, occurs when there is photodegradability, a breakdown by sunlight. But since most trash bags are buried in landfills, the benefits of photodegradability are questionable. Thus, the government has stated that one way to improve deceptive advertising claims is to eliminate false or misleading information.

23b. Illogical Comparisons
1. Compared to my statistics class, economics is very easy.
2. We know that people who are regularly exposed to second-hand smoke are more likely to get lung cancer than people who are not exposed.
3. When I want to feel depressed, I compare the lifestyles of the rich and famous to my own.
4. After our small plane levelled out at 1500 metres, the flight became as smooth as that of any commercial airliner.
5. We are all convinced of the durability of Canadian products, even though they cost a lot to make.
6. What I've discovered in my interviews is that children under 10 tend to have musical tastes like those of their parents.
7. The Beatles have sold more albums than any other musical group.
8. The features of one laptop are pretty much the same as those of every computer in the same price range.
9. There is no better time to observe mob behaviour than during major sporting events

Chapter 24 Dangling and Misplaced Modifiers

24a. Dangling Modifiers
1. The Library of Parliament has finally been renovated. <u>Considered an architectural treasure</u>, tourists love to see this perfect example of Victorian gothic style. The library is the only part of the parliament buildings to

have survived the fire of 1916. During the renovation, the copper roofs have required specific attention, as they are considered to be national symbols. <u>Weather-beaten and suffering from the elements</u>, it was in the 1950s that the roofs had last been replaced. <u>Now a bright copper colour</u>, chemical oxidation over the next twenty years will give the new roofs a familiar green tinge. Then, <u>to protect the library from moisture damage</u>, the roofs will have moisture barriers and a new drainage system. Though exposure to the elements cannot be prevented, the rebuilt roofs should fare better than their predecessors, thanks to modern technology. <u>Looking better than ever</u>, our Canadian heritage is well represented.

24b. Misplaced Modifiers

1.   The Canadian Food Inspection Agency has been <u>recently</u> busy with mad cow disease <u>in its investigations</u>. May 2003 saw the first case that Canada has reported <u>in recent years</u>. As a result of the findings, several ranches in Alberta, B.C., and Saskatchewan were quarantined as a precaution. At that time, 1,400 cows were <u>nearly</u> slaughtered so they could be tested for the disease. DNA evidence revealed that an infected cow had been born in Canada, so many countries, including the United States, banned the import of Canadian beef and dairy products <u>in written declarations</u>. Because of the Canadian Food Inspection Agency's aggressive program <u>now</u>, any cow has been destroyed <u>that might have been exposed to the disease</u>. Today, Canada is again considered a minimal-risk region for mad cow disease, and cattle sales are <u>at home and abroad</u> once again lucrative.

24a-24b. Additional Modifier Exercises

Responses will vary, but possible revisions are provided here.
1. Scientists have discovered Cro-Magnon man, being the first to use primitive tools, was more human than ape.
2. Using a large flashlight, Mari stunned the pit bull.
3. After working at the dairy for twenty years, Jerome was devastated by his dismissal.
4. You need a lot of strength to open a new jar of pickles.
5. Brendan found a woman's emerald bracelet on the floor of the language lab.
6. The greenbelt offered a convenient shortcut for anyone looking for a quick way through the subdivision.
7. For the past three winters we have had hardly any snow.
8. On the top shelf of the refrigerator, Kelly found a pie baked by her mother.
9. The township decided that nobody except local ratepayers could dump anything at the landfill.

PART SIX

Chapter 25 Nouns and Pronouns

25a-b. Nouns and Noun Endings

1. Sports fanatics are spending large sums of money these <u>days</u> to purchase sports memorabilia. In fact, says one of the <u>industry's</u> <u>spokespeople</u>, it is a $100 million-a-year obsession. Buyers look for <u>scorecards</u>, stadium <u>seats</u>, autographed baseball <u>bats</u>, <u>pucks</u>, even <u>children's</u> clothing that belonged to all-time greats such as Tiger Woods. One of <u>Woods'</u> personal <u>letters</u> recently sold for over $10,000. Since Joe Lewis, a famous boxer, kept many of his old <u>mouthguards</u>, collectors are now paying over $2000 for boxed sets of <u>Lewis's</u> <u>mouthguards</u>. There are plenty of <u>websites</u> to keep <u>collectors</u> informed about the availability of various <u>items</u> of interest. A sociology professor at a major university who has begun a study of this phenomenon reports that yearly increases in prices are staggering. One of the most valuable <u>transactions</u> ever was a 1979 Wayne Gretzky rookie card that sold for $80,000. In fact, Gretzky memorabilia is some of the most popular—and therefore the most expensive—sports <u>treasures</u> around. Prices can only keep going up since there are so many sports <u>fanatics</u> looking to buy.

25c. Noun Phrases

1. a
2. d
3. b
4. a
5. e
6. a
7. c

25d. Pronouns

The business of sports collectibles has become so profitable that <u>it</u> has attracted con artists <u>who</u> manage to forge and sell bogus items. The forgeries have become such big business, in fact, that many con artists help <u>one another</u> and have developed a large network of bogus items. These items include fake Steve Nash signatures and imitation press box pins. <u>Anyone</u> <u>who</u> is in the memorabilia business can spot <u>these</u> as forgeries and fakes, but sports fans are often too enthusiastic to take the time to have <u>their</u> purchases checked by an expert. As a result, <u>they</u> often allow <u>themselves</u> to be conned. A lot of junk from people's attics is also cluttering the market. When <u>someone</u> finds yellowed pages from 1929 sports sections in <u>her</u> scrapbook, <u>she</u> may think <u>she</u> has an expensive treasure. Flea markets overflow with antiques <u>which</u> may or may not be worth anything. But if <u>someone</u> is willing to pay large sums of money, <u>who</u> can say whether that autographed photo or threadbare jersey is or is not a treasure worth collecting? With a market where buyers will pay over $1,000 for one of Sidney Crosby's old sweaters, <u>it</u> is worth <u>it</u> to clean out those old attics and scrapbooks.

25e. Pronoun Case

1. In 2004, Thomas C. Douglas was voted "the Greatest Canadian" on a nationally televised contest organized by the CBC. Tommy Douglas is considered a hero by <u>those</u> Canadians <u>who</u> admire his idealism and commitment to socialism. <u>His</u> greatest accomplishment is probably that the NDP and <u>he</u> introduced universal public health care to Canada. However, Douglas was condemned at the time by doctors <u>who</u> felt his plan was a disadvantage to <u>them</u>. Many doctors went as far as to say that Douglas intended to bring in foreign doctors <u>whom</u> the government would pay less but <u>who</u> would offer lower standards of care. Canadians are also grateful for <u>him</u> for arranging to pass the Saskatchewan Bill of Rights, <u>which</u> broke new ground as it protected both fundamental freedoms and equality rights. He served as an MP and MLA, but Canadians remember <u>him</u> best as leader of the NDP. Douglas died of cancer in 1986 at the age of 81. Even now, many scholars continue to concern <u>themselves</u> with the impact Douglas had on Canadian society.

3. Fall break was over, and the research assignment was due the next day, so Ross asked Lucy if she wanted to go to the library with Amy and <u>him</u>. The instructor had told the class that the students <u>who</u> made high grades on the midterm exam would be those <u>who</u> had read the assignments and completed all the homework. Ross had missed that lecture. When the girls and <u>he</u> reached the reference room, they saw several classmates <u>who</u> they

could work with. They asked their friends, "Who has finished the assignment?" They were surprised that all the other students were already finished and heading to Tim Hortons. It was clear to Ross that a long night lay ahead for them. The next day, Ross asked the instructor, "Please give Lucy, Amy, and me one more day to finish the research assignment." But the teacher said it wouldn't be fair to the rest of the students who had all worked hard, so Ross and they learned the hard way not to procrastinate.

25f. Pronoun Reference

1.　　When Benjamin Franklin discovered electricity in thunderclouds, he sparked a controversy that still has no clear answer. How do clouds become electrified in the first place? To this day they haven't been able to adequately explain how it contains such incredible amounts of electricity that a stroke of lightning can contain about 100 million volts. One researcher who wants to find some answers flies his plane into storms to measure electric fields and ice particle changes. It's bumpy work, he says, especially if there are large hailstones because it can damage the plane and the measuring equipment. On one trip they noticed that in sections of clouds where water and ice mix, the measuring devices picked up indications of strong charge separation. The answer may be that in a certain temperature range, the temperature can cause the charge separation. Another factor may be a kind of soft hail called "graupel," pea-sized particles that can look like miniature raspberries. They form when droplets of supercooled water collide, freezing together instantly. Ice crystals then bounce off the growing graupel, building up a charge from the friction just as you build up a static electricity charge when you scuff your feet across the carpet. When they are carried to different parts of the cloud, the result is a separation of the positively and negatively charged particles. Then, when the electrical difference between the ground and the sky becomes great enough, everyone should haul his or her kite in.

Chapter 26 Verbs

26a. Verb Phrases

1.　　Some scientists are saying that a buildup of carbon dioxide and other greenhouse gases in the atmosphere causes global warming. But another group of scientists argue that we should study the data more carefully before any firm conclusions are drawn. While scientists generally agree that an unchecked accumulation of greenhouse gases will cause changes, no one knows when it will start, how much will happen, or how rapidly it will occur. The most widely accepted estimate is that there will be a rise in the earth's average temperature as early as 2050. This could bring rising sea levels and severe droughts in some areas. But no one knows yet how clouds and the ocean's ability to absorb heat will affect this. When scientists understand this better, projections can be revised.

26b. Verb Forms

1.　　The evidence that global warming has started is not very strong. Some scientists believe that the concentration of carbon dioxide has increased over 25 percent since the early 1800s, but other scientists point to the fact that the average global temperature has risen by no more than a half degree Celsius. Even that rise is questionable since there was a cooling period from 1940 to 1970 that caused forecasters to predict a return to the ice ages. Therefore, to act on predictions by passing laws that restrict or ban the use of fossil fuels may be hasty; nevertheless, conserving energy, banning harmful chlorofluorocarbons, and planting more trees to absorb carbon dioxide from the air makes sense. Many industries are also acting more responsibly and are reducing hazardous emissions from their factories.

26c. Verb Tense

1.　　For over 130 years, future members of the RCMP have attended a training program at Depot Division in Regina, Saskatchewan. From the outside, the RCMP headquarters looks like an ordinary building, but it is considered a Canadian heritage site. Today, Depot is considered one of the top tourist sites in North America. In May 2007, the Government of Canada and the Government of Saskatchewan opened the multi-million-dollar RCMP Heritage Centre, which features several permanent exhibits about the history of the Mounties. The exhibit titles include "Serving All of Canada," "Cracking the Case," and "Duty Calls." Tourists are amazed at a sculptural procession called the "March of the Mounties," which runs the length of the main exhibit hall and is

30 metres long. One of the main purposes of the Heritage Centre <u>is</u> to educate Canadians about the role the RCMP <u>plays</u> in protecting our country and in creating the Canadian identity.

2.   Last year an average of 8,500 men and women <u>wrote</u> the RCMP entrance exam, but only 1,984 cadets <u>were</u> selected. At Depot, the RCMP training academy, cadets <u>took</u> part in an intense 24-week program, in both English and French. The cadets <u>were</u> divided into troops of 32 members. Together the cadets <u>moved</u> through the program, which usually <u>began</u> with scenario training and role play. The emphasis <u>was</u> on real-life situations. For that reason, much of the training <u>took</u> place in a model detachment where cadets <u>developed</u> hands-on skills. Cadets <u>acted</u> out arrests. Training also <u>incorporated</u> problem-solving, lectures, panel discussions, and community interaction. The program <u>was</u> gruelling, but once training <u>was</u> complete, cadets <u>were</u> prepared to begin their careers as RCMP officers.

26d. Verb Voice

1.   Our nation's capital borders (<u>active</u>) two provinces, Ontario and Quebec. Like many cities that are built (<u>passive</u>) on a river, the bulk of the population is divided (<u>passive</u>) on both sides. The bigger city is Ottawa, but over one-half of the city's employees reside (<u>active</u>) in Gatineau, the city on the other side of the river. Problems are created (<u>passive</u>) when it comes time to finance projects that will benefit (<u>active</u>) both cities. In 1959, the National Capital Commission was founded (<u>passive</u>) to organize such projects. Today, the NCC organizes (<u>active</u>) projects that impact both Gatineau and Ottawa. Advocates of the NCC say (<u>active</u>) that the organization makes (<u>active</u>) events and tourism run more smoothly. Opponents claim that the NCC is a waste of money and that residents of Ottawa who pay higher taxes are taken advantage of (<u>passive</u>) by residents of Gatineau. Beautification of the capital region is a hot-button issue, with many people now advocating (<u>active</u>) for the disbanding of the NCC.

26e. Verb Mood

1.   Singles bars and dating services are thriving (<u>declarative</u>), but there are always new approaches. In commercial dating services, one new approach that may be cheaper (<u>subjunctive</u>) than the standard videotaped interviews is the lunch-date service. For less than $50 a month, the company promises (<u>declarative</u>) three lunch dates a month. People are paired on the basis of simple criteria gathered from brief interviews that might last (<u>subjunctive</u>) less than five minutes. The company sets up the lunch date, and the participants take it from there. "Meet (<u>imperative</u>) new people," says the advertising brochure, "and enjoy (<u>imperative</u>) some interesting little restaurants." Since Statistics Canada puts (<u>declarative</u>) the number of never-married Canadians at 1.1 million and growing, these new twists on dating services may well prosper (<u>subjunctive</u>).

26f. Modal Verbs

1.   When western products began appearing in Moscow, city officials worried that the signs and advertising for these products <u>might</u> make (<u>could possibly make</u>) Moscow look less Russian. A law recently passed in Moscow warns that all stores and businesses <u>must</u> display (<u>need to display</u>) signs in Russian or at least change them into the Cyrillic alphabet. This has caused many businesses to contact the city inspector because of questions they have. For example, one businessman wondered whether he <u>should</u> change (<u>is obliged to change</u>) the letters in the label for the Puma running shoes that he sells. He was concerned that changing the letters from English to Russian <u>might</u> make (<u>has the possibility of making</u>) the shoes less popular. The problem became confusing because the new law does not forbid foreign words but does require the Russian sign to be bigger than the one in English. Different stores found different solutions. An American cosmetics company, Estée Lauder, announced that it <u>would</u> put (<u>strongly intended to put</u>) one sign in Russian on the awning and another sign in English in the windows. Despite all the questions and worries, the inspector in charge of enforcing this rule will be (<u>is going to be</u>) very strict about checking on foreign signs.

Chapter 27 Modifiers

27a. Adjectives and Adverbs

1.   For <u>many</u> people, the <u>crossword</u> puzzle in the <u>daily</u> paper is one of life's <u>little</u> pleasures. Some say it is <u>more like</u> one of life's frustrations. While <u>puzzle</u> books <u>conveniently</u> include the answers in the back, newspapers usually print the answers in the <u>next</u> day's edition. Now there is a <u>quicker</u> answer. <u>Some</u> publications have an <u>automated</u> solution. Readers can dial an <u>800</u> service for <u>instant</u> answers. <u>This</u> service is

free to callers and is paid for by advertisers who sponsor each day's puzzle. The advertiser can run a small advertisement beside the puzzle or include a ten-second message that callers must listen to before the answers are given. Other newspapers handle this differently. For their puzzles, there is a special number, and callers have to pay for all requests for clues. These services are actually a major breakthrough for frustrated puzzle-doers who have been used to waiting until the next day.

27b. Comparisons

1. larger
2. largest
3. more exciting
4. most enjoyable
5. user-friendliest (or most user-friendly)
6. better
7. best
8. worst
9. farther
10. most expensive
11. older (or elder)

27c. Prepositions

1. It was once so normal to pour ketchup on everything that it was considered everyone's favourite condiment. Now salsa has replaced it as the preferred choice between the two at many restaurants. Salsa, which means "sauce" in Spanish, is defined as any fresh-tasting, chunky mixture, usually made with tomatoes, chilies, onions, and other seasonings. Although salsa used to be associated with Mexican cooking, it is now being used for a variety of foods not particularly Mexican. The popularity of salsa is apparently part of the current food trend as we become more interested in spicier foods. In 1988, only 16 percent of households in North America bought salsa. In two years, that figure was up to 36 percent, and the market continues to grow at a very fast rate. A marketing information company notes that salsas and picantes—which are different from salsas because they are thinner—account for about two-thirds of this market, a category that also includes taco and enchilada sauces. As the market expands, so do the choices. The simplest salsas are based on chopped tomatoes and chilies, and the types of chilies determine how hot the particular type of salsa is. Cookbooks with a variety of recipes indicate the preference of some people to make their salsas at home. Salsas are one of the few popular snack foods that are fat-free or nearly so, and many are made without preservatives, two characteristics that may contribute to their popularity now that people are interested in healthier eating. Riding on this wave of popularity are the new fruit salsas, made with peaches, pineapples, and so on, and vegetable salsas, made with pinto beans, corn, and black-eyed peas. Other varieties will surely appear as the market keeps expanding in the future.

27d. Clauses

1. (If you are a sociable writer who lives in a big city and likes informal gatherings), you may want to join a local writer's club. A typical group might meet bi-weekly or monthly at a local Second Cup or Starbucks, (where members can discuss their craft in comfort). Writers come from all professions; they can be doctors, professors, salespersons in shoes stores, tax attorneys, shipping clerks, or teenagers (who write as a hobby and would like to improve). Others are professionals [(who have published a little or a lot) but (who still like to hear other opinions) (before they submit a manuscript)]. All of these writers share a love of the written word. (Because they know how helpful it can be to get feedback), they willingly read each other's writing and offer constructive criticism.

2. There are an estimated 50,000 magicians in North America. Most are amateurs who enjoy magic as a hobby (adjective clause). These amateurs often have elaborate equipment although their only audience is usually their friends and relatives (adverb clause). Some specialize in the small card, coin, and rope tricks that are always popular (adjective clause). Purists call this intimate "close-up" magic the only real magic because it relies so heavily on a person's manual dexterity (adverb clause). Because people seem to prefer to be fooled face to face (adverb clause), this close-up magic is also offered by professional magicians who perform at birthday parties and trade shows (adjective clause). One psychologist, who is also a magician (adjective clause), says that when something is done under people's noses (adverb clause), it's more magical. It's much more

203

elusive. The spectacular effects of magic done on television don't seem to impress people quite so much. Whatever the cause may be (adverb clause), amateur magicians will keep buying those sponge balls, decks of cards, special coins, and paper flowers.

27e. Reduced Clauses

One of the most deadly offensives for Canada during World War II was the raid on Dieppe, a sea-borne mission across the English Channel made by two Canadian brigades and other units. While being a British operation, the Battle of Dieppe, also known as Operation Jubilee, depended on almost 5,000 Canadian troops. After considering all the variables, one of the commanding officers, Lt.-Gen. McNaughton, claimed that chances for success were good, providing luck was on the side of the Canadians. This was not to be. Despite the fine weather, the troops, landing on the beaches around 5 a.m., met with a determined and well-organized counter-attack. By 9 a.m. they were beginning to lose ground badly after fighting valiantly. The decision was taken to retreat, evacuating any commando not already trapped behind the German lines. Of the Canadians making up the attacking force, 993 were killed, 586 were wounded, and 1,874 were taken prisoner. Long debated for its heavy cost in lives, the raid on Dieppe is still seen as a testament to Canadian bravery.

Chapter 28 Essential and Non-essential Modifiers

1. Responses will vary, but one possible revision is provided here. New sentences have been italicized.

    French teachers in elementary schools across Canada who want their students to speak more now have a new, groundbreaking program to help them. AIM is developed by a group of educators who want to introduce French in a way which will get the students involved. *Students say it is a lot of fun.* This program is being used to get children to speak with ease. *The program incorporates singing, story telling, and hand-gestures.* Students seem to enjoy the songs and stories, and the hand-gestures help them remember new vocabulary. At the end of a unit, students can put on a play that goes with the story for the rest of the school. Once students learn the vocabulary with confidence, teachers can use other exercises to expand the children's knowledge of French. AIM is rapidly growing, with over 3500 schools across Canada using it to teach French.

PART SEVEN

Chapter 30 Nouns and Determiners

30a. Nouns

In Canadian supermarkets, new <u>products</u> and <u>produce</u> are constantly being added to the shelves. Children are attracted to new snack foods, and adults are frequently tempted to buy items with <u>information</u> about health benefits. To increase consumer <u>confidence</u> in package labelling, the Canadian Food Inspection Agency has announced new <u>guidelines</u> for various claims food manufacturers add to their labels. Products that are advertised as "low <u>fat</u> " have to provide <u>evidence</u> on the label and meet new government <u>standards</u>. For items that appeal to children, the amount of <u>sugar</u> must be clearly indicated. Particularly helpful are the new regulations on serving size because consumers have become very conscious of the amount of <u>protein</u> and <u>fat</u> that they eat as well as the number of <u>calories</u>.

30b. Determiners

1.   In northern India there is <u>a</u> conflict between wildlife officials and Gujjar herders of water buffalo. <u>The</u> Indian Government wants to turn the area into a national park, to be called the Fajaji National Park, but for the last ten years, local water buffalo herders refuse to move off the land. The Gujjars keep herding their water buffalo, despite warnings that the animals are eating up too <u>much</u> of the vegetation and that soon there will be <u>few</u> areas that have not been destroyed by the herding. Several decades ago, the Gujjars agreed to migrate every summer to give the forests a chance to grow again, but communities in the areas they migrated to refused to accept the Gujjars because they needed <u>the</u> land for their own grazing, and they didn't have <u>enough</u> land to share. As a result, the Gujjars now stay in the forest throughout <u>the</u> year. Government officials keep on warning of <u>the</u> dangers of erosion in the forests where Gujjar herding has stripped the land. While <u>some</u> environmental groups say that these forest dwellers have as much right to the land as the animals, other groups support the government's attempt to move the Gujjars. The continued grazing by water buffalo risks using up the <u>few</u> food sources of elephants and other animals. Government officials plan to make <u>an</u> offer to the Gujjars to move them to settlements on the edge of the forests and to have them feed their animals in stalls. Park officials want to find <u>a</u> solution soon because they say that both the park and the Gujjars will suffer if the present situation continues.

3.   After winding down twenty miles of dirt road in Mtunthama, Malawi, (no article) visitors will come upon the well-kept lawns and gardens of (the) Kamuzu Academy, one of (no article) Africa's most unusual schools. Here, on four hundred acres of well-trimmed lands is (a) school dedicated to classical scholarship. (The) school was founded by President Hastings Kamuzu Banda, the ruler of Malawi since it won its independence from (the) British in 1964. Originally, Dr. Banda studied at (a) Scottish missionary school in Malawi and went on to study in (no article) South Africa, (the) United States of America, and (no article) Britain, where he acquired (a) medical degree and (a) love of Latin and Greek, as well as a strong attraction to the classical emphasis of the elite British schools. When Dr. Banda returned to Malawi, he wanted to copy (the) architecture and curriculum of Eton and other British boarding schools. Some critics in opposition to Dr. Banda say that (the) academy is not appropriate in their country where ordinary schools often do not have (no article) textbooks and where more than two-thirds of (the) population are illiterate. However, defenders of the school point out that the school is not elite in choosing its students. Children are accepted without regard to their family's wealth or position. Each year 35,000 students take (an) exam to try to gain entrance to the school, which accepts about eighty new students (a) year. Once accepted, all students are required to take four years of (no article) Latin and four years of (no article) ancient Greek, along with (no article) English, (no article) mathematics, and (a) history course about Africa. Most graduates go on to university and then take jobs in (the) Malawi civil service.

Chapter 31 Verb Patterns

31a. Auxiliary and Main Verbs

1.   Wines have been <u>produced</u> in the Champagne district of France for over two thousand years. However, a monk who <u>was</u> named Dom Perignon is <u>acknowledged</u> as the father of the delightful celebratory wine known as champagne. He may <u>have</u> brought international fame to the district as early as the 1660s. Dom Perignon, who <u>has</u> given his name to one of the priciest brands, did <u>develop</u> and refine his methods in a local monastery. There he used to <u>induce</u> and <u>control</u> the second fermentation that might sometimes <u>occur</u> naturally in the bottle during

warm weather. The resulting carbon dioxide which <u>is</u> trapped in the bottle will <u>give</u> "bubbly" its characteristic effervescence. Generations of champagne makers would <u>have</u> refined these techniques until methods were <u>standardized</u> in the 1880s. Now only the product which <u>is</u> made and bottled in the Champagne district there is supposed to be <u>called</u> champagne. But wine makers in the Niagara district <u>are</u> now producing a variety of sparkling wine called Champagnade that may well <u>outsell</u> the French product in Canada.

31c. Verbs with –ing and to + verb forms

In Canada, students are expected <u>to learn</u> more than just the subject matter they are beginning <u>to study</u>. Their teachers urge them <u>to examine</u> a subject thoroughly, <u>to ask</u> questions, and even <u>to disagree</u> with the opinions of experts if there is good reason. Educators recommend <u>taking</u> such an approach because it helps students <u>to become</u> better thinkers. Students not familiar with the Canadian school system may avoid <u>practising</u> such critical thinking skills. They may not have been allowed <u>to question</u> an authority or the written word in their country as a sign of disrespect. Another problem that such students may encounter in Canada involves <u>writing</u> assignments. In Canada students are often asked to <u>choose</u> topics that argue accepted ideas. Students from other countries often need <u>to be</u> encouraged <u>to express</u> opinions without <u>apologizing</u> because they may have been forbidden <u>to discuss</u> controversial topics in high school. Students' cultural backgrounds certainly affect many aspects of academic life, including how they approach the educational experience.

Chapter 32 Idiomatic Usage

32b. Idiomatic Prepositions
2. Halifax, Nova Scotia, <u>in</u> the spring of 1851 was a prosperous, diverse city. Halifax was characterized <u>by</u> a tremendous energy and pursuit <u>of</u> success that one would expect <u>in</u> a growing city where the population had just passed 20,000 people. Halifax was somewhat <u>of</u> a cultural mosaic <u>with</u> a constantly increasing number of new residents. Many were <u>from</u> the United States, black loyalists who had fought <u>for</u> the British in the War of 1812. There were also significant numbers of immigrants <u>from</u> Germany, Scotland, and Ireland who had been attracted <u>by</u> the booming fishing market. The 1830s brought <u>to</u> the previously Protestant Halifax a large number of Irish Catholics whose crops had been devastated <u>by</u> the potato famine. There were of course large numbers of French and British descendants who had been living <u>in</u> conflict there since the 1700s. Inevitably, competition and distrust existed <u>between</u> the various groups, but gradually these were worked out <u>in</u> most cases.

32c. Idiomatic Sentence Patterns with *There, Here*, and *It*
1. a. There were many people complaining about the delays at the airport.
  b. There was some kind of thick slime oozing from the pipe.
  c. There is a lot of work that needs to be done to complete the project.
  d. There is more than one correct answer to this question.

2. a. It was a shame that Eve missed the last bus home.
  b. It is very convenient to use my new tablet PC.
  c. It is impossible not to be embarrassed when you make a mistake.
  d. It is the French exam, not the English exam, that is on Tuesday.

32d. Unidiomatic Repetition
a. Students in my class <u>they</u> are looking forward to the upcoming vacation.
b. My tuition is being paid by an uncle I worked for <u>him</u> after graduating from high school.
c. Although the accident was minor, <u>yet</u> the driver was still taken to hospital.
d. My teacher found the book that I left <u>it</u> in the classroom.
e. The apartment building where I live <u>there</u> has two swimming pools.
f. My neighbour returned the lawnmower that he had borrowed <u>it</u>.
g. For many people, <u>they</u> will not walk under a ladder even if they say they are not superstitious.
h. The pie in the refrigerator <u>it</u> is for tonight's party.
i. The book drop where library books are returned <u>there</u> is full.
j. In some parts of Saudi Arabia, ten years may pass <u>there</u> without rain.

32e. Positions for Modifiers
a.   Three eager new students quickly entered the classroom.
b.   Her favourite Japanese food is sushi.
c.   The two little girls were very easily frightened.
d.   Almost everyone experiences intense homesickness sometimes.
e.   I suddenly spotted a huge black menacing cloud.

PART EIGHT

Chapter 33 End Punctuation

"Do you see that green area to the left of the river we are flying over?" said the pilot to the passengers as the commercial jet flew over southern Alberta. Continued the pilot, "That's my grandfather's ranch. I often visited there as a kid." Public-address systems in commercial planes are now being used by pilots to enliven their passengers' flights. Some pilots are opposed to this practice because they see it as a distraction. Says one seasoned veteran, "Our task is to fly the plane, not amuse the passengers." But others disagree. Interesting, informative comments can put nervous passengers more at ease and can shorten a long flight. For those pilots interested in making such public-address announcements, there is now a book put together by an ex-pilot pinpointing more than 1,200 historical and little-known places of interest on a collection of highway maps. The maps are overlaid with the flight paths used by commercial pilots. Are you flying between El Paso, Texas, and Las Vegas, New Mexico? If so, then look for the site of the Berringer Crater, where a meteor hit with such force 22,000 years ago that it killed all animal and plant life within 100 miles! Thousands of these maps have been sold, with more frequent fliers than pilots doing the buying. "We are learning an awful lot about territory we thought we knew!" says one frequent flier who takes her book with her on every flight. Another customer reports, "I bought one for my uncle who hates airplanes, and he now actually enjoys his flights." The book is obviously a success. Who can disagree with an author who predicts, "Soon, there will be such books in the pocket of every seat in every commercial flight"?

Chapter 34 Commas

34a-b. Commas in Series and Lists; Commas with Adjectives

When he died in August 2007, Paul MacCready was well known as an award-winning aeronautical engineer, the founder of several important scientific companies, and an innovative, ingenious inventor. He created his first transportation device before graduating from junior high school—a model flying machine that could take off, fly, and land with little power. MacCready was recognized as scientifically gifted from an early, precocious age. He trained as a pilot at the end of WWII, then completed a bachelor's degree in physics, a master's degree in physics, and a Ph.D. in aeronautics by the time he was twenty-seven. MacCready became known in the 1970s for a series of fanciful functional aircraft that relied on unusual energy sources like electric power, solar power, and even human power. The three most impressive of MacCready's inventions have ended up in the Smithsonian Institute: the Gossamer Condor, the Gossamer Albatross, and the solar-powered lightweight car called the Sunraycer. One of his more spectacular creations—a life-sized flying plastic replica of a pterodactyl—was developed for a Smithsonian IMAX production in 1985.

34c. Commas in Compound Sentences

1.   In 1977 the flight of the little airplane, the Gossamer Condor, did not look very impressive, but it was indeed an historic flight. With wings of foam, balsa wood, and Mylar, the plane designed by Paul MacCready floated slowly and gracefully over the San Joaquin Valley and covered a mile or so in about eight minutes. What made it so historic was that the pilot was pedalling. The Gossamer Condor was only the first of MacCready's pedal-powered planes, and two years later the plane's successor, the Gossamer Albatross, crossed the English Channel. Some people say that MacCready is really the brains behind these inventions, but others feel that he receives undue credit for the work that others on the development teams do. However, MacCready was the first to use his observations of how birds fly, so his supporters feel that he is the genius who made human-powered flight possible. Other inventors were taking the conventional approach of trying to reduce drag as much as possible because they thought this approach would be the answer. The approaches of other inventors were to streamline their aircraft, or they tried to incorporate ways to increase the horsepower. Only MacCready applied the principle of vastly increasing the wing area and used materials to keep the overall weight down. The result was an aircraft that needed only the power output of a good bicyclist, and the Gossamer Condor now has a place of honor next to the *Spirit of St. Louis* in the Smithsonian Institute.

34d. Commas after Introductory Words, Phrases, and Clauses

1.   Having won prizes with his first human-powered plane, Paul MacCready went on to build a faster and more powerful pedal-powered plane, the Gossamer Albatross. In less than two years after his first success,

MacCready's second pedal-powered plane departed from Folkestone, England, in June, 1979, bound for France. Expecting the flight to take about two hours, MacCready allotted just enough water for the pilot to drink. The flight team who prepared the plane and assisted the pilot on the ground waited several weeks for the kind of calm weather that was needed. Consequently, the pilot took off, expecting to reach France before his endurance and the water gave out. But a head wind blew up soon after the pilot was aloft. An hour and a half later, he was only two-thirds of the way to France, and his legs were cramping from all the pedalling. Because everyone was sure they had to give up the attempt, the flight team was ready to hook a towline to the craft that would haul it ashore. Tired and about to give up, the pilot knew he had to gain altitude to get hooked to the towline. As he climbed, he found less wind and was able to press on. Almost three hours later, the pilot touched down at Cape Gris-Nez, in France, a minute short of his theoretical exhaustion point. The Gossamer Albatross had crossed the English Channel, powered only by the pilot.

34e. Commas with Essential and Non-essential Words, Phrases, and Clauses
1.   After designing human-powered planes, Paul MacCready, a prize-winning inventor, went on to design a solar-powered plane. MacCready, however, realized that solar cells as an energy source for planes do not make any practical sense. But MacCready, who had long sympathized with environmental concerns, hoped to demonstrate that solar power has an important part in the world's energy future. Those who see solar energy as merely a minor source of energy for the future downplay the importance of such demonstrations. Others think solar power has simply not been adequately developed for practical use. The solar-powered plane that MacCready designed flew from Paris to the coast of England in 1981, cruising at 441 mph at an altitude of 11,000 feet. The plane, called the Solar Challenger, provided the stepping stone to MacCready's next flying machine, the Sunraycer, a solar-powered car.

34f-h. Comma Conventions; Other Uses for Commas; Inappropriate Commas
The Sunraycer, which is a solar-powered lightweight car, was built to compete in the 1987 Race Across Australia. Designed by Paul MacCready, the car won the race from Darwin to Adelaide_ and is now in the Smithsonian Institute. With a total weight of 365 pounds, the car has a power output of about 1.8 horsepower at noon on a bright day, and it gets the electric power equivalent of 500 miles to the gallon. The Sunraycer, which presently holds the solar-powered speed record of 48.7 mph, averaged a little over 40 mph for much of the race. The car is so light_that when it made turns during testing, it often seemed in danger of blowing over. The engineers who worked on the Sunraycer_ended up putting two little ears on the top. "We're not sure why they work," said one engineer, "though they seem to help." In some ways the Sunraycer is not a prototype of electric cars for commercial use_ because the Sunraycer has bicycle-thin wheels, a driver's seat that requires the driver to lie flat, and very weak acceleration. However, many of Sunraycer's features were carried over into the electric car developed by General Motors. Like the Sunraycer, the GM car uses alternating current_ and can, therefore, get better performance. If electric-powered cars become widely popular in the future, Paul MacCready can certainly be credited with having helped save the environment.

34a-h Review of Comma Usage
1.   introductory element, address
2.   no commas
3.   appositive
4.   adjectives in series
5.   non-essential clause
6.   appositive, introductory element
7.   introductory element, date
8.   no commas
9.   compound sentence
10.   interrupter, contrasting element

Chapter 35 Semicolons

1.   Junk mail used to be confined to print on paper; now it is appearing in people's mailboxes on CDs or videodisks. Companies in the direct-mail business are now marketing inexpensive cardboard videodisks that can carry a variety of messages; such as audiovisual advertisements, promotional premiums, and educational or

training aids. Some companies are switching to this form of direct-mail advertising because it is relatively cheap; in addition, it presents messages more vividly on screens than print advertising can on paper. Informational videos can be sent to prospective customers, and advertisers feature their product in the video. Says the spokesperson for one cereal company, "We are interested in promoting good nutritional habits"; as might be expected, the balanced diet pictured in the video will include that company's cereal. Printed instructions on merchandise are often confusing; consequently, some manufacturers are also switching to disposable videodisks to deliver information included with the merchandise. The cardboard videodisks are relatively cheap to manufacture and cheap to mail. They are certainly more convenient than the promotional packets sent by companies that have relied on enclosing sample packets of toothpaste, aspirin, or cereal; mail advertisers who send bulky envelopes of coupons; and companies who want to entice customers with big brochures of vacation places, hotels, and tours. The disposable videodisk is certainly growing in popularity as an advertising medium.

Chapter 36 Colons

1.   Deciding what to do after graduation is challenging for many university students. For this reason, many Canadian universities have established career centres where students can research employment opportunities. At the centres, students can do things such as meet with a career counsellor, practise their interview skills, and revamp their résumés. Here is what one counsellor has to say: "When it comes to choosing a profession, many students do not know what opportunities are available to them, and this lack of knowledge is exactly what the career centres seek to remedy." Some of the most important resources at the centres are the personality tests which assess students' skills and weaknesses and their likes and dislikes. After taking such a test, students can see more clearly what sorts of fields they might excel in. Many career centres also offer workshops and career fairs. Some students who have visited the campus career centres are thrilled with what they have learned. Just researching what career choices are available has helped many students decide what sort of future they want.

Chapter 37 Quotation Marks

1.   "Why am I fatter than my sister-in-law? I eat less," complained a woman being studied by a team of researchers. She explained that she repeatedly went on diets when her sister-in-law didn't. But the woman continues to weigh more. Researchers are finding out that heredity, in addition to lifestyle, exerts a strong influence on people's weight. By studying identical and fraternal twins, research teams are finding that brothers and sisters end up with similar body weights whether or not they are raised in different families. In the *Journal of Genetics*, Dr. Albert Skinnerd writes, "When the biological parents are fat, there is an 80 percent chance that their children will also be overweight" (234). "Does this mean that my brother and I are doomed to be fat?" asked one overweight twin in the study. Since some sets of twins tend to transform extra calories into fat while other sets of twins tend to convert extra calories into muscle, one scientist concluded that "genes do seem to have something to do with the amount you gain when you overeat." Some unsuccessful dieters may be relieved to know that their failed diets aren't a matter of failed willpower. "It is really a matter of metabolism," reports another doctor doing research in this field. But that does not mean that low-fat diets and exercise should be given up. " 'Quit' is not a word in my vocabulary," says one constant dieter who manages to maintain a reasonable weight by means of careful eating and plenty of exercise, despite a tendency for extra pounds.

Chapter 38 Apostrophes

1.   In the game of baseball, batting slumps are one of a player's worst nightmares. When they are doing well, players attribute their successes to mysterious minor occurrences around them that then become habits the players keep up. After a game in which one baseball player who was wearing an old helmet with its side dented hit two triples, a home run, and a single, the player continued to wear that helmet for the rest of the season. Warding off evil spirits through superstitions is another thing baseball players do. One player always wears his favourite T-shirt under his team's jersey. Another won't wear a jersey with any 6's in his player's number. Batting coaches spend hours watching videotapes with slumping players, trying to find what's causing the

problem. They examine the player's batting stance or swing, but this does n't always provide useful clues. Some slumps happen when batters begin to worry too much about their misses and about everyone else's successes. But one coach thinks otherwise. He notes that some players start making adjustments when they've hit a double and want to hit farther or when a certain unusual pitch connected well with their bats. Players in their 30's complain of a different kind of slump. One bad day, says one over-30 player, may mean he is losing it, that his age has begun to take its toll. A batter's life is n't as easy as some people think it is.

Chapter 39 Other Punctuation

1.   Which oils are good for us to eat? A study of thirty-nine participants on a reduced-fat diet looked at the benefits of consuming olive oil and/or corn oil. Which oil is more beneficial in influencing lipoprotein levels? This question is important because high-density lipoprotein (HDL) is considered a beneficial form of cholesterol that helps remove the more dangerous low-density lipoproteins from the body. In a study published in an article, "Two Healthy Oils for Human Consumption" (*Diet and Health News* 36 [2008]: 22-36), researchers report that the participants first spent twelve weeks on a diet that included olive oil and then another twelve weeks on a corn oil diet. The results (which were widely reported) indicated that neither diet resulted in lower levels of HDL. Therefore, a diet of olive oil and/or corn oil can safely accompany a reduced-fat diet. For those who self-select the oils they use in their diet, the choice is probably a matter of taste—or cost.

PART NINE

Chapters 40, 41, 42 Capitals, Abbreviations, and Numbers

1.   Today, Toronto is one of Canada's largest and most diverse cities. Not many tourists realize that this <u>m</u>odern <u>c</u>apital can also take them on a visit to Canada's past. Visitors interested in the <u>h</u>istory of Toronto have many hidden away places where they can find relics of the past. They should make a point of visiting <u>h</u>istoric Fort York, the location of the Battle of York during the war of <u>1812</u>. Fort York is considered the birthplace of modern Toronto. Here, tourists can visit Canada's largest collection of original War of 1812 <u>b</u>uildings, take tours, and watch <u>m</u>usket, <u>d</u>rill, and <u>m</u>usic demonstrations. On Victoria Day and Canada Day, the Fort comes to life with nearly <u>a hundred</u> costumed actors playing the parts of soldiers, servants, leaders <u>and so on</u>. The fort is almost <u>three</u> kilometres long with <u>twelve</u> restored buildings, including the <u>b</u>arracks. Another educational visit would be to the home of William Lyon Mackenzie, one of Canada's most notorious and celebrated figures, whose involvement in the <u>1837</u> Upper Canada <u>R</u>ebellion was made famous in James Reaney's children's book *The Boy with an R in His Hand*. Many tourists do not realize that many of the places mentioned in Reaney's novel are still part of the Toronto landscape, most significantly Mackenzie's <u>h</u>ome. This <u>G</u>reek-revival rowhouse was also where Mackenzie, at the time an outspoken newspaperman, put his newspaper to press. Today, visitors can come to its location at 82 Bond <u>Street</u>, south of Dundas <u>Street</u>, and visit what the home would have been like. It is <u>two</u> storeys tall, and the pressroom is built on at the back. Finally, tourists looking to go back in <u>t</u>ime should visit St. James Cathedral, es<u>t</u>ablished <u>in</u> 1793. Though the church suffered <u>two</u> major fires, parts of the original still endure. This church was used as a <u>h</u>ospital during the <u>W</u>ar of 1812 and has existed on the same spot since before the <u>t</u>own of York became Toronto. Indeed, though Toronto's <u>d</u>owntown is incredibly modern, tourists who look carefully can still find reminders of an exciting past.

Chapter 43 Underlining/Italics

1. a. U
     b. U
     c. Q
     d. U
     e. U
     f. Q
     g. Q
     h. U
     i. U
     j. Q
     k. U
     l. Q
     m. U
     n. Q
     o. U
     p. U
     q. U
     r. U
     s. Q
     t. U

Chapter 44 Spelling

44c. Proofreading

    Inventors of gadgets for automobiles <u>haven't</u> always been successful with <u>their</u> inventions. But we can see from some <u>of</u> these inventions that people have been looking for ways to make cars more <u>functional</u>, better looking, and more fun to drive. <u>For</u> example, we now have <u>elegant</u> and sophisticated ways to <u>hear</u> music in <u>our</u> cars, but some of the earlier ways to add music to driving seem a bit odd now. In the <u>1920s</u>, Daniel Young <u>received</u> a patent for an organ he invented for use in automobiles. He built organ keyboards that could be <u>accommodated</u> to <u>the</u> back of the front seat so that people <u>riding</u> in the back could play the organ to entertain <u>themselves</u>. This may have been a good idea, <u>except</u> for one thing. The roads of that time, <u>unfortunately</u>, were so bumpy and uneven that the sounds <u>produced</u> by the organ when the car was moving <u>were anything</u> but beautiful. Another <u>terrific</u> idea that didn't make it was Leander Pelton's patent for a car that could be parked by standing it on end. Instead of a back bumper, he <u>built</u> a vertical platform with <u>rollers</u> attached. When parking the Vertical-Park Car, the driver needed to tip the car back onto <u>the</u> platform. <u>Then</u> he could just shove the car into any <u>appropriately</u> sized space. To <u>perform</u> this task, however, was a <u>bit difficult</u> as Pelton never quite explained how the car was to be <u>tipped</u> from <u>horizontal</u> to vertical and back down again. A <u>different</u> problem was that Pelton didn't <u>provide</u> any way to keep gasoline, water, and oil from spilling once the car was up on its <u>parking</u> rollers. But the <u>government</u> gave him a patent; he simply couldn't get anyone to <u>manufacture</u> his Vertical-Park <u>Car</u>. Another invention that never made it was designed by Joseph Grant in 1926—an <u>automobile washing</u> machine. The <u>machine</u> didn't wash cars, but it <u>supposedly</u> washed clothes. Grant's invention <u>consisted</u> of a tub and paddles that bolted to the car's <u>running</u> boards. <u>When</u> the tub was filled with water, soap, and <u>dirty</u> clothes, the bouncing of the car over <u>rough</u> roads provided all the power and <u>agitation</u> necessary to clean a load of dirty clothes. For <u>really</u> dirty <u>loads</u>, an extra twenty miles or so of driving was <u>recommended</u>.

44d. Some Spelling Guidelines

1. a. believe
    b. yield
    c. seize
    d. height
    e. foreign
    f. weird
    g. field
    h. handkerchief
    i. deceive
    j. leisure
    k. neither
    l. ceiling
    m. niece
    n. neighbour
    o. vein

2. a. napping
    b. jewellery
    c. starred
    d. tapping
    e. writing
    f. referred
    g. stripped
    h. occurrence
    i. beginning
    j. benefited
    k. shopping
    l. omitted

44f. Sound-Alike Words (Homonyms)

1. a. except
    b. accept
    c. affected
    d. effect
    e. all together
    f. It's
    g. it's

h. its

i. passed

j. than

k. then

l. then

m. there, their

n. to, too

o. where, were

p. who's

q. you're, your

r. advice, buying

s. site

t. quite

u. stationary

v. already

w. all right

x. any one

y. all together

PART TEN

Chapter 47 Searching for Information

47a. Choosing Primary and Secondary Sources
1. secondary
2. primary
3. secondary
4. secondary
5. primary
6. secondary
7. primary

PART ELEVEN

Chapter 53 Documenting in MLA Style

2. Works Cited

Baer, Walter S. "Telecommunications Technology in the 1990s," *Computer Science* June 1994: 152+.
    Dialog 102, 0346142.

Jamieson, Valerie. "Atomic Logic." *New Scientist* 9 Feb. 2008: 44-47.

Newlove, John. "Ride Off Any Horizon." *15 Canadian Poets x 3*. Ed. Gary Geddes. 4th ed., Don Mills:
    Oxford UP, 2001. 229-32.

Nickerson, Norma Polovitz, and Paula Kerr. *Snapshots: An Introduction to Tourism*. Toronto: Pearson
    Prentice Hall, 2007

Raphael, Dennis. *Poverty and Policy in Canada: Implications for Health and Quality of Life*. Toronto:
    Canadian Scholars Press, 2007.

Rutherdale, Robert Allen, and Magdalena Fahrni, eds. *Creating Postwar Canada: Community, Diversity,
    and Dissent, 1945-75*. Vancouver: UBC Press, 2008.

Shakespeare, William. *Hamlet*. CD-ROM. CMCReSearch, 1989.

Shapiro, Marla. "Interview." *Canada A.M.,* CTV 7 Feb., 2008.

PART TWELVE

Chapter 54 Documenting in APA Style

2. References

Baer, W. S. (1994, June). Telecommunications Technology in the 1990s. *Computer Science,* 152+. Retrieved from Dialog 102, 0346142.

Canadians on the Move (2000). In S. Girvan (Ed.) *Canadian global almanac* (p. 67) Toronto: Macmillan Canada.

Jamieson, V. (2008, 9 February). Atomic Logic. *New Scientist* 9 Feb. 2008: 44-47.

Nickerson, N. P., & Kerr, P. *Snapshots: An introduction to tourism.* Toronto: Pearson Prentice Hall.

Raphael, D. (2007) *Poverty and policy in Canada: Implications for health and quality of life.* Toronto: Canadian Scholars Press.

Rutherdale, R. A., & Fahrni, M. (Eds.). (2008). *Creating postwar Canada: Community, diversity, and dissent, 1945-75.* Vancouver: UBC Press.

Shakespeare, W. (1989). *Hamlet.* [CD-ROM]. CMCReSearch.

Shapiro, M. (2008, Feb. 7). Interview. *Canada a.m.* CTV.

Chapter 55 Documenting in Other Styles

1.   C
2.   E
3.   A
4.   B
5.   D

NOTES

NOTES

NOTES